BROKEN
to
RESTORED

FINDING YOURSELF BY LOSING YOURSELF

MELVINA PEKA

http://www.melvinapekaministries.com

Free Bonus #1 Download your personal meditation

BROKEN
To
RESTORED

A seed lies dormant with a promise in its belly and sprouts only when hidden in the deep dark dirt. Like a seed, we also need the right environment and time to bring forth the purpose God has placed inside us.

MELVINA PEKA

© **Copyright** 2019 – Melvina Peka

All rights reserved. Except as permitted by written permission, no part of this publication may be reproduced, distributed, or transmitted in any form or by any means, or stored in a database or retrieval system.

For Worldwide Distribution, Printed in Australia.

www.melvina.global

melvinaministry@gmail.com

Please note I am not using capitals for lucifer and satan- as I choose not to give him any importance in my life.

Scripture quotations marked (ESV) are from The ESV® Bible (The Holy Bible, English Standard Version®), copyright © 2001 by Crossway, a publishing ministry of Good News Publishers. Used by permission. All rights reserved."

Scriptures quotations marked NIV, taken from the HOLY BIBLE, NEW INTERNATIONAL VERSION®. NIV®. Copyright © 1973, 1978, 1984 by International Bible Society. Used by permission of Zondervan. All rights reserved worldwide.

Scripture quotations marked NKJV, taken from the New King James Version®. Copyright © 1982 by Thomas Nelson. Used by permission. All rights reserved.

Scripture quotations marked (GNT) are from the Good News Translation in Today's English Version- Second Edition Copyright © 1992 by American Bible Society. Used by Permission.

Disclaimer: All information contained within this publication is designed to provide helpful information on the subjects discussed and not in any way intended as a substitute for individual advice. The reader should seek their own professional advice in matters relating to their health and wellbeing. The intent is to offer information and choices, recognizing that we all have our own viewpoints and circumstances.

Should any reader choose to make use of the information contained therein, this is their choice.

The publisher, companies or author disclaims any liability, loss or risk, personal or otherwise, to any person reading or following the information or applying the contents in this book.

Dedication

I would like to dedicate *Broken to Restored* to my daughter, Payal.

You are so much like me and have had your own share of struggles. I enjoy seeing you grow into the beautiful woman that you have become, overcoming your challenges and embracing all that God has for you.

I love you Payal and am proud of you. Keep pressing on, your greater is coming!

CONTENTS

Dedication

Preface

Acknowledgments

Introduction 9

Chapter One: The Scene 23

Chapter Two: Finding yourself 57

Chapter Three: Comfort or Vision 85

Chapter Four: Envy is a Deception 145

Chapter Five: The Mind is the Powerhouse. 167

Chapter Six: When God is Quiet 189

Chapter Seven: Daring Faith 195

Chapter Eight: Wilderness, the road to Destiny 219

Chapter Nine: Transition 251

Chapter Ten: When God Calls You, Get Ready for a Fight
 273

Chapter Eleven: Fear is a thief 281

Chapter Twelve: Jesus Feels Your Pain 291

Chapter Thirteen: Being Like the Father 311

Chapter Fourteen: The stones will Praise Him 321

Chapter Fifteen: Loosed woman 329

Chapter Sixteen: The Fragrance of the Broken 339
Accepting Jesus 349

Preface

We all hold onto something that we cherish for several reasons and even though it may no longer be essential for us to preserve it, we refuse to discard it. Like an item of clothing that no longer fits us, or an old car sitting in the garage that we are hoping to fix.

Likewise, we also hold onto some memories from our past in the silent corner of our mind, and every now and then, it may whisper to us, beckoning us to return to the world we left behind.

It is when we have the courage to face the truth and are able to forgive others and ourselves, we are truly able to release our past and embrace the new. Like a trapeze in a circus who must let go of the bar behind them to grab hold of the bar ahead of them, we also need to let go of the past hurts and people who have broken us, to grasp onto the future because everything God has for us is ahead of us, not behind. We ought to only look back far enough to worship God for bringing us out and leading us to His plan, because in order to lay hold of His plans for our life we must let go of things of our past. Past has a way of showing up when we least expect.

God expects us to apprehend every thought that speaks in our life that is negative and discriminatory and is not of Him and substitute it with thoughts of empowerment and hope. No one else can do it for us. We ourselves have to open our mouth and speak words that give life and not death. His written words spoken over our lives brings life to our dead areas, to our diseases and hopelessness.

Acknowledgments

I want to honor and thank the Lord, my childhood best friend; without you, I would not have discovered my calling. Thank you, Lord, for literally finding and saving me from myself, for being the healer of my broken heart; for being the lifter of my head and for calling me "your buttercup."

I revere you, oh Lord for transforming my life; from bringing me from the back to the front, for who am I that you would even look at me, my shame, my brokenness, and my nothingness, and so carefully you put it all together like a Mosaic birthing a ministry.

It is an absolute pleasure and privilege to serve you and to be able to share the joy and healing that you have given me with others like me.

Thank you to Frank, my husband, my second-best friend. I am so honored to be your wife, handpicked gift to me from God himself. Thank you for not giving up on me through the trials and challenges of life, and for dreaming with me. Thank you for your patience and for listening to the many sermons I preached in the lounge with you as my only congregation; for loving me unconditionally and holding me up in the Lord each time I was falling. Thank You for believing in the call of God on my life, when no one else did. Your love, your patience, and your support mean so much to me. You have been my prayer partner interceding for me day and night. Your prayers protected the walls and birthed this ministry. I could not have done this without you. I love you very much.

Thank you, God, for my three beautiful children. You have been my strength, propelling me to fly higher. You brought purpose to my life and kept me from giving up. I love each one of you so much.

My mum and my dad, thank you for giving me Jesus so early in my life. You taught me to put my trust in God no matter what. If it wasn't for this strong foundation in my life so early, I would not be here today. Thank you for your love that was always there for me even when I made bad decisions and choices. You both are in Heaven cheering me on now.

If only you knew your little girl is ministering to thousands from the little seed, you planted in me as a young child by sending me out with the missionaries to evangelize in the village. I am honored to be your daughter. Thank you, Pastor Nola Waterman and your team of prayer warriors, you have been there for me since the day I walked into your church broken, bleeding and lost. You embraced and loved me and helped me grow into the confident, strong woman of faith that I have become. I thank you for the prophetic word you gave me that confirmed God's vision for my life.

I thank you, Sharon King, for believing in my calling and for steering me in the right direction. Thank you for the seed you planted in my ministry so early when it was just a promise in my belly. You have helped me in so many ways and I will always be grateful to you.

I especially thank the late Pastor Barrimah and Pastor Mrs. Grace Addo of The All Nations Christian Centre, Reservoir, Melbourne in seeing in me God's calling and giving me a chance to fly. I remain grateful.

To all my friends and families; over the years you stood by me. You saw me in good times and in bad times. You all know who you are. You all have enriched my life in more ways than you can imagine. I love you all.

Free Bonus meditation download click below or visit us on http://www.melvinapekaministries.com

https://documentcloud.adobe.com/link/track?uri=urn%3Aaaid%3Ascds%3AUS%3A7bcdbb72-f1c8-4b89-9032-7e7c5cb6d860

To book Melvina for a **FREE** 30-minute consultation, fill out and email the form below to book your seat. We will contact you for a Skype chat.

MPM   Membership Form

Please complete this application to join Mel's mailing list so that you can be notified of promotions and free stuff.

First Name _____

Last Name _____

Email _____

Country & City _____

Please scan and email to melvinaministry@gmail.com

https://www.instagram.com/melvinapeka/
https://twitter.com/melvinapeka?s=09
https://www.melvinapekaministries.com/mels-blogs
https://m.facebook.com/melvinapekaministries/
https://www.youtube.com/channel/UCKN3_bea0oEd3sH0d4qJXGg

Introduction

God has aligned our steps and our paths cross for reasons. Everyone we meet and everyone who comes in our lives is there for a purpose.

Nothing is by chance and nothing is wasted in God. Every day we fall down, and every day we must get up, shake the dust off us, learn the lessons it taught us and keep walking toward our destiny.

Alabaster Jars are usually thick and dense long-necked vessels. These Jars were made by the Egyptians of valuable marbles and precious stones and often contained oils and perfumes owned only by the wealthy.

The story of the Alabaster Jar is outlined in the Bible in Luke 7:36-38 demonstrating wordless worship by a worldly woman with an ungodly past who gatecrashes a party with an act that upsets others in attendance. The audaciousness of this woman to make such a fearless effort to get close to a man in a public forum was unheard of. She came uninvited and unveiled to a function where the affluent were gathered and Jesus was the chief guest of honor. Her act makes all the religious leaders annoyed.

Some say this mysterious unnamed lady was of a promiscuous character, sexually disgraced, a prostitute who lured men to her bed with her sweet lips, curvaceous body and extravagant perfumes. People say everyone in this world 'sells' themselves out for money in some form or way, be it for business or personal! However, for this woman, it appeared that she was no longer content selling herself. She wanted a career change. We can leave a bad situation but how do we take the situation out of us? When we have lived in a depraved situation for too long, it comes inside of us, controls us, becomes a stronghold, holds us at a ransom! This lady could not take the burden anymore, the jeering of people, the guilt and backlash that came with her profession, and desired to get out of it all! It was a good sign because when we have reached a point of despair where our situation becomes intolerable, it brings out a distinctive kind of strength and innate confidence that makes us push forward no matter what. When this occurs then there is no holding back. For this lady, no amount of money or gifts were compensating for the emotional heaviness that she was carrying.

She was the principal topic of conversation among the women of the town whose husbands might have visited her bed. Matthew and Mark in the Bible described her as an unnamed woman from Bethany. John, however, identifies her as Mary of Bethany, while Luke who loves to give details of events writes of a "woman of the city, who was a sinner", who bathes Jesus' tired, dusty, dirty, feet with a mixture of perfume and her tears, wiping it with her long black hair and kissing his feet with her lips as an act of worship.

When I was growing up, I often heard from mothers and grandmothers that a girl's hair was her glory and for this reason, many would prefer girls hair to be longer. This lady laid her glory at Jesus' feet, which means everything she had, everything she ever wanted to be, all her dreams and desires and worshipped Him without taking into consideration where she was and who was observing. There is a kind of praise that activates the blessings God has dispatched which is hovering in the atmosphere being held by satanic forces (Daniel 10:13) and unless we turn on the floodgates of our worship and release our faith, it will not reach us.

"Do not be afraid, Daniel. Since the ***first day*** *that you set your mind to gain understanding and to humble yourself before your God,* ***your words were heard,*** and I have come in response to them. But the prince of the

Persian kingdom resisted me twenty-one days. Then Michael, one of the chief princes, came to help me, because I was detained there with the king of Persia," (Daniel 10:12-13 NIV). If you have been wondering why your prayers are not being heard, God made ears so He hears even our sigh, but satan, the enemy resists the delivery of our blessing and that is why we cannot give up easily just because we have prayed once or twice. When we persist in the most discouraging situations and declare positive affirmations, it releases power to restore.

This lady with the Alabaster Jar was not on the guest list of individuals who were attending the party. There was no assigned seat reserved for her and no one expected her. But she had a place in Jesus' heart. From behind the crowd, she silently advanced toward Jesus. She was a desperate and persistent woman who left all her pretense behind. Have you ever felt like quitting, perhaps your dead-end job or your undesired circumstances, desperate, depleted, depreciated, empty and invisible, at a breaking point of your life, that you needed the Lion of Judah to roar in your circumstances like never before and break that wall of the mortgage, or that problem standing like a wall in front of you?

She came from an era where the church would not accept people who looked different, ladies who were bleeding, wore clothes that did not fit their church dress code or those whose profession portfolio did not fit their welcome list. People who they alleged were from a certain type of sinful background were not welcome. The Bible says that this lady was a 'known' sinner. She was famous but for the wrong reasons, her reputation was terrible, she was a known call girl, a 'hooker', someone who exchanged sex with money or something of value. However, she did not have two faces and did not hide behind any mask. People thought they knew her, and they judged her by her profession. You know how some people think they know us and reserve the right to critique, judge and condemn us just because they have lived next door to us for few years, or because they follow us on social media, or because we went out with them a few times. We may live with people in the same house or even sleep in the same bed with them for many years, but we still don't really know them. We may sit with the same person at work for years and eat with them in the lunch room, but we don't really know them. We don't know if they are being abused at home, if they are in a domestic violence situation. We put on an act to hide our truth. Isn't it always the people who are closest to you hurt you the most, people you believed would stand beside you during your trial, or when God is lifting you up, they would celebrate with you, support you through your project, but they stand indifferent because they don't understand your calling and decide to scrutinize you? They dissect everything you say and do. There is a reason they are against you and grouping together to destroy you;

because you have something of value. No one comes to steal in an empty house. Stay away from these types of people who don't have a vision themselves and are not going anywhere spiritually and professionally. Surround yourself with people who can influence your life, promote you and encourage you, not the ones who shred you to pieces and throw you to the vultures.

A girl from my school had committed suicide. Everyone was distraught. It affected the whole community. Some said they knew her very well, they sat with her, ate with her, walked with her to school but never saw the signs of depression or that she needed help. How well do we really know anyone? We may grow up in the same home, and think we know each other but do we really? We are all performers in life, we put up an exterior, we may smile and nod appropriately but inside we could be hurting and angry. Difficult times usually bring out the truth in people, the bad or the good. It will show you who they really are, whether they are for you or against you. Either way, your trust is in God who is the one who starts and finishes your story. If they hate you, it does not affect God's calling in your life. God knows you because He fashioned you intricately in your mother's womb.

Someone right there in our own home or at our work place in our very own cubical could be depressed and thinking of suicide or something else, but we are not able to see or hear their cry for help. People have gone on a shooting spree and killed children in school yards, and these are the people from our neighbourhood, someone we knew, but did we really 'see' them? We walked past them at the shopping mall or sat with them in the bus, our eyes crossed at the counter, we smiled but we did not hear their cry for help or see their tears of emotional pain.

This lady was crying for help and no one heard her. She was well known by men and women. Many men used her services, but they did not know her, the real her. What drew a known sinner to walk many miles, past all those interrogative eyes and spiteful whispers to come and see a religious leader in a special private assembly? Her heart was full of emotions she had been holding back for a long time. She was undervalued for an extended amount of time; her callings and gifts were lying dormant for too long. People had whispered about her for many years, but it was time now to awaken her destiny. She found the one who held the key to her destiny. She did not allow her profession or her past choices to define her. With tears like dewdrops falling on Jesus' feet washing the dust off his feet, she whispered, *"against you and you alone have I sinned."* Jesus extended a hand to her head. She didn't belong to the exclusive club of the priesthood or the rich, but she did not care. She came with all her excess baggage of emotions and her past sinful life, a life of sex, smoking, drinking, call girl attitude, no pretense and unashamedly she offloaded it at Jesus' feet. She emptied her bank account and bought the most expensive gift she could buy, an alabaster jar of perfume that only the rich could afford. She clasped against her broken heart her elaborate gift of the perfume and courageously marched out of her dwelling and strode past the gossips and hateful verbal dialects to find Jesus, the miracle worker. No town gossip or hateful words could stop her. This was her one chance to find freedom.

She probably knew the identity of every other man present there who were howling at her. She had the opportunity to shut them all up by revealing each of their bedroom secrets, but she kept her mouth fastened because this moment was not for them, this was her moment to receive, a holy moment. When we worship, we can turn any place into a holy ground as Joshua did in the book of Joshua falling to the ground he worshiped God right there in the battleground. Are you in a battlefield right now, and it is threatening to strip you down, don't worry or fear, turn on your worship? Water of worship drowned the pigs in the Bible.

The Lady with the Alabaster Jar came for one purpose, to free herself, to find redemption from the one Man who really knew her. Her life of immorality weighed heavily on her, wherever she went, the rumour went ahead of her. No amount of perfume or washing could clean her. She had no words that could articulate what she was feeling in her heart; her tears spoke for her as she poured her livelihood of perfume on Him, the one man whose gaze beheld her real beauty that others failed to capture. Before she could tell him her story, Jesus forgave her. Grace invaded her life in the middle of a public forum.

When our heart is filled with sorrow and we have no words to express our pain or find the words to pray, our tears become our prayer. God's grace is available to everyone, even to those who we think do not deserve it.

Our hurts and unforgiveness weigh us down and inhibit our growth and prevent us from soaring high. There will always be haters, but we cannot allow their chatter to enter us because it will drown us. God has plenty of grace to go around for everyone even when others reject us, shame us and hurt us. He forgives them just as He forgives us. Who are we to hold a grudge then?

Chapter One
The Scene

I would like to invite you to take a stroll with me to this fake scene where the lady with the Alabaster Jar gatecrashes an influential private party. The affluent people of the town are in this exclusive high-profile function and amongst the invited guests is the mayor of the town, the respected religious leaders, the well-known medical specialists and the surgeons, the business people, the lecturers, the bankers and the actors, the politicians, and other well to do A-list individuals. The buzz in town is that Jesus is visiting as the principal guest. The social media is trending Jesus is in town with hashtags. The news media vehicle is parked on the street two blocks down as locating a parking spot was impossible due to the overbearing crowd. There is a multitude of people everywhere trying to catch a glimpse and to take a photo of Jesus. Some have even brought their sick families and friends for healing and there are people in wheelchairs and other mobility aids flocking in. People have come from far away villages and from other nearby towns and while some are sitting on the pavements and on the grass outside, others are trying to climb shrubs and trees to sneak a peek at Jesus. The camera people and the reporters are making the best of this open possibility of filming life videos, taking photographs and directing interviews of individual guests.

There is a great deal of noise of people vocalizing outside while on the inside refreshments are being served and *'selfies'* are being taken with Jesus and with other influential people. Several guests are doing a live Facebook video while others are posting on Instagram and other social media.

Suddenly there is a moment of silence in the air and everything changes. A female arrives pushing through the assembly unannounced, with one hand grasping her veil as women were enjoined to cover their head in communal places and with another hand embracing against her bosom as if nursing a baby, a marble bottle. She hastily moves past the gatekeepers and other notable people and in one motion throws herself at Jesus' feet before anyone could halt her. Some men hurried to push her away. She protests while Jesus elevates his hand in a motion to leave her alone. The television and media personnel were busy broadcasting her every movement. She pours the costly perfume from the alabaster Jar on Jesus' feet and then she stoops to wipe his feet with her lengthy black silky hair, weeping. The fragrance of the scent was so pungent that it pervaded the room and drifted outside. The shawl that covered her hair lay flaccid on the floor beside Jesus' feet as she sobbed desperately succumbing herself at His feet. It was an accepted traditional custom of that time for all women to have their head covered in the community and the audacity of this sinful woman to make such a public show of herself without her head covering was unpardonable.

There is one praise that makes you forget where you are and who you are or how you look. Her veil slithered off her head, but she did not care because Jesus provided the covering for her. His Grace sheltered her.

Can you envisage the facial expression on all those spectators? Several people were shouting disagreeably at her human action of seeking mercy at Jesus' feet and attempted to remove her, while some others proceeded to the party as if nothing had occurred. A moment of muteness for others as they observed this astonishing act by a strange woman, then the whispering and gossip commenced. Some told her off discourteously while others looked on in bewilderment and with blended feelings of revulsion, abhorrence, amazement, and anger.

This is what it would have looked like if it occurred in this century, but this happened in a period when it was impermissible for women to touch a man in a public domain in this manner, yet this bold unidentified woman broke all religious beliefs, restrictions and social obstruction in pursuit of something that no man could give her. She desired something far greater than their money could buy. No acquisition or medium of exchange could satisfy her deep hunger of being loved and forgiven. She wanted redemption and freedom from all the guilt and emotional ache she was living with for an extended period. She yearned for love, for someone to see her as a person and not just a sex object. She wanted someone to see past her beguiling eyes and her thick eyelashes, her beautiful fair skin and past her curvaceous body and behold the woman she was on the inside. Many men visited her bed and enjoyed her body, but no one visited her soul, touched her heart, read her feelings and saw her emotions.

An untamed worship has the power to break all barriers

In her one act of adoration at Jesus' feet, she represented all women who have been giving of themselves in assorted roles all their lives, even when afflicted and weary, they continued to give. A woman, a mother often gives of herself silently to her family and those around her and no one comprehends the cost of her giving. No one takes time to see the actual person who has given up their own dreams and desires to make other people's dreams come true. Sometimes they have had to dim their own light so that others could shine theirs brighter. This lady who had a reputation unbolts the door for all of us in her one demonstration and escorts us inside to witness an untamed worship. She shows us what a wild worship costs and what it looks like, and that no matter where we have been or what we have done, there is redemption at Jesus' feet.

This nameless woman humbles herself at the feet of Jesus, the miracle worker, the Master and restorer of all things, seeking acceptance and forgiveness. The narrative does not tell us what led her to the route of harlotry, but no young girl chooses prostitution as an occupation eagerly. Circumstances in life makes people do things they would not ordinarily do and then they get caught up in the web unable to find their way out. This unidentified lady yearned for freedom from the guilty conscience, from the disgrace, from feeling dirty all the time and from the sadness that came with this type of enterprise. Every night she entertained a different man, but she could not keep any, or make anyone fall in love with her. She fabricated her smile but deep down she craved for real love, a home, and a family. She secretly envied other women who hated her but did not know how much she wanted to be like them, to have a home and children.

The people who witnessed this episode condemned her open demonstration of emotion for a man she did not know. They powerfully opposed to Jesus having anything to do with an adulteress. The confidence of this wicked woman to touch the master's feet in this manner was a disgrace to the tradition and customs of the culture. Her act in public was not only unsolicited but prohibited. Let's assume that some men who were disapproving of her open act of worship in this fashion and shouted at her the loudest and attempted to remove her, knew her very well intimately from her services rendered to them. Isn't it often the ones you thought you knew and would stand by you in the challenging times of your life that disappoint, leave and betray you to the enemies, throw you to the predators without one-second thought? People judge you because you do not fit into their tiny box of how things ought to be done. Their own darkness cannot handle your light, because you are not ordinary. They judged this woman because her way of worship was different from theirs. When she was nourishing their sickening sexual habits and shining the light for them, they welcomed her into their bed and their wallets but the moment she decided to pursue her own true purpose and desired something more than they could give her, they condemned her. People will be quick to discard you and talk behind your back the minute you decide to leave them to make something of yourself. They don't like you because they don't understand why you must show your scar to everyone, share your testimony of where God found you, leave them to chase after some vision and destiny. They liked you better when you were broke and doing crazy things with them. Now they don't know who you are because all you do is talk about God and the Bible and your testimonies.

Now that you are trying to improve your life and go after something better, they are intimidated by who you are becoming and they fabricate lies, generate rumors to make themselves feel important. They don't know what God has whispered to you, they question your calling and pull you down to their level. God did not tell others what He told Moses, Jeremiah, Jonah or Noah. Your relationship with God is all that matters. He is very good at shutting the mouth of lions and tigers who prey on you. He is the fourth man in your fiery furnace and when you come out, there will be no odor of smoke on you.

Pay no consideration to their chatter, because God is uplifting you to a level where they cannot accompany you. He is lifting you up to a rock that is higher than you. He is the rock of ages the mighty powerful God who has placed something inside of you and in due time it will come out. God has to ensure we will be able to handle all the new challenges that come with being in our season of blessing. When He has elevated us, there will be many who will talk about us saying they knew us from when we were in high school or when they worked with us or shared house with us. If God is digging you deep down, it is only because He is devising a plan to elevate you and where He is taking you, it is necessary to cut some people loose in your life because they will only drag you back to your past and pull you down with them and suffocate your calling. There will be people in our circle who will accuse us and doubt our calling; we don't have to justify anything to them. They have been sent to sieve us. Stand tall in what God has called you to do and don't give up just because they are against it. Don't give in to their demands just because your light is convicting them. God would not have held you up before Satan as He did Job if He did not love you and believe in you to do the project. When God is about to take you to the next level, there is always challenges that come as a trial of faith, do it without complaining. Don't worry about your haters, they will be disposed of!

This woman left everyone and was not embarrassed to go after what she desired. She did not care about the etiquette of the rich and famous. She lived an exclusive lifestyle, in her own terms even if she did not choose to live a life of sin initially. She was not one of those women who settled for less. She appeared to be someone who dared to draw outside of the line. The kind of woman who did not allow the babble and whisper of people to get in the way of her destiny. Perhaps she figured out what could be worse, living a life that was less than God's best for her or breaking all pious rules and social guidelines to go after her dream despite all the name calling and hatred of people.

There is a praise; wild, fierce and penetrating that permeates through all the cells of the body, touches every organ, fiber and nerve and destroys sicknesses, breaks every chain, interrupts poverty, and lack. A kind of praise that brings down Heavenly resources and healing like no other. Her praise broke some strongholds and chains in her life that day and released Heavenly blessings.

God calls us to worship in this manner as if our life and our children's legacy, our marriage, and our finances depended on it. He expects us to bring to Him our emptiness, our pain, and sorrows, for the Bible says to worship Him in spirit and truth (see John 4:24). Jesus calls us to transport to Him whatever our truth is today, however dreadful and painful it may be, convey to Him and worship Him, He can handle the ugliness of our past.

Worship is an act of sacrifice, a giving of oneself or one thing that is most valuable in gratitude of something someone has done that was undeserving. God gave us His son, a part of Himself while we were still sinners, undeserving and unworthy, but He did it because of His love for us, who He calls His children.

Jesus communicates to the people who were provoked by her actions and tells them to leave her alone, that she had done nothing deceptive. He recognized her movements as an exceptional act of reverence.

The Pharisees talked amongst themselves and Simon who was the host said to 'himself', "If this man were a prophet, he would know who is touching him and what kind of woman she is--that she is a sinner," (Luke 7:39 NIV).

How did Simon know so much about her unless he was also her client?

Jesus 'heard' Simon's thought. Jesus who could read Simon's unspoken thoughts and knows the end from the beginning knew everything about this lady even what others did not know.

Jesus looking at Simon the accuser, recites a story about two men who owed money to a wealthy man, one owed a great deal of money and the other a smaller amount. The lender forgave them both because they could not pay their debt. Jesus asked Simon, "Who was forgiven more?" "The one, I suppose, for whom he canceled the larger debt," Simon answered. Jesus glanced at the sinful woman *while speaking* to Simon, "Do you see this woman? I entered your house; you gave me no water for my feet, but she has wet my feet with her tears and wiped them with her hair. You gave me no kiss, but from the time I came in, she has not ceased to kiss my feet. You did not anoint my head with oil, but she has anointed my feet with ointment. Therefore, I tell you, her sin, which are many, are forgiven- for he who is given little, loves little," Luke 7 ESV.

God forgives all sins

How many times, we characterize different types of sin; the sin which is small is okay to forgive while the sin which is too big should not be forgiven. We can forgive a liar, but not a rapist or a murderer because their sin is too big, yet we can murder a baby in the mother's uterus and say it is okay. We call it little sin and big sin, but any type of sin is a sin, big or small. In God's eyes raping someone is the same as stealing a dollar. It is a sin and Jesus paid the price for both, for ALL sins, there is no big and small sin.

We become all righteous and holy in our religious outfit and forget where the blood found us when we begin to label others who are still trying to find their way. If it was not for the Lord, we would still be in that sin. We are hasty in judging someone but do not realize that they may be trying to overcome their sin and instead of helping them we label and judge them. The people condemned the lady with the Alabaster Jar; they perceived her as sinful by the method she was using to earn her living. But the men who used her services did not conceive their own actions as sinful. Simon labeled this lady sinful as if he was sinless and had never done anything wrong.

This lady was familiar with her reputation in town and what people named her. She was not there to deny her wrongdoings or make excuses for her choices. She made a radical choice to meet Jesus and to ask Him for His mercy and she went all the way in, without holding back anything to display her extraordinary love. Radical people may set up a daring front even when they have been disappointed and broken inside, they are often very faithful in love and give all of themselves.

Be careful when you judge radical people; just because they are wild in a way you don't understand, doesn't mean God cannot use them. God used radical people like Paul, who was an activist killing Christians when he encountered Jesus on the road to Damascus and his life changed. From killing the Christians, he converted to one of the most fundamental followers of Jesus (see Acts).

Radical people are the ones who push boundaries, they don't settle for less. The timid, the conservative can't do what this lady with the Alabaster Jar had done. She appeared to be someone who would do anything to get what she wanted. She wanted freedom from her past and she knew exactly who was able to give it to her.

There is a kind of praise that breaks through all barriers and hers was one of those distinctive praises. Deep-seated faith that escalates into an astonishing act, intensifying on the inside like a fire uncontained, ready to burn every obstacle, break all barricades, like a tidal wave sweeping through everything without holding back. I don't care who is watching kind of faith. Faith that gives you an inner confidence to get dressed every morning for work before you even get the job. The kind of faith that makes you feel and move your fingers on a piano before you get the piano. The kind that dried up a fig tree and made the deceased ambulate. Sometimes when we are restless in our circumstance, it is a sign that we have outgrown our territory, it is time to move out of our comfort zone and take that step forward toward the promised land. Time to spread those wings, get out of the nest to fly on our own. Crazy faith that gets you to act out all the way even when people laugh at you and families think you have gone crazy like Noah. In the book of Genesis, people thought Noah was crazy when he set out to build an ark. He had a radical faith that said, I would rather look crazy for God and be in His plan than do something that looks good and fits into your expectations about me and step out of Gods plan for my life.

Jesus calls all of us to come to Him unapologetically. His love can handle all our shame, our game, and all our messes. Nothing we can do or have done that He hasn't died for. In Him, we find redemption, love, and peace and most importantly rest. This lady did not appear to have harmony in her soul. She seemed to be exhausted from her lifestyle, making everyone else happy but living an unfulfilled life. She was living less than her potential, it wasn't her best life and she knew Jesus could give her that. No man could satisfy the hunger within her soul. No amount of sex or perfumes and expensive gifts could fill the void in her life the way Jesus could.

I often consider the reason she remained unidentified is to reach out to all women who have been rejected, had lived a lonely life feeling unloved and invisible, disgraced and humiliated so that we all can transcribe our own name in her place and make it our own story. We all have been accused by the devil for the things we have done in the past or was done to us, like rape or abuse. We may have come from a shameful and sinful past, did some things we are not proud of, scammed and stole things that belonged to others or any other form of transgression can identify with her act of worship because like her we too have been forgiven much.

What you have is enough

Often religion has expected only good, neatly dressed people in the presence of God, people with great marriages and well-behaved children even if it was a lie. People who they perceived as sinful like this lady with the Alabaster Jar, a prostitute, specifically the ones who practiced openly, people who looked and behaved differently, maybe cross-dressed or had a different sexual orientation, people who dressed outrageously and had perhaps spiky hairdo, tongue pierced, with tattoos all over, bleeding women were not welcome in church. The Bible says, (see Mark 2:17), that Jesus came for the lowly, the discarded and the broken and said that only the sick needed the doctor. Our suffering, brokenness, and shame are the things that draw Jesus closer to us because He too was broken and shamed for us. If anyone who understands our messed-up life, it's Jesus. He was sent by God to help us and to bring us all closer to Him.

Regardless of what has happened to us and where we have been, the reward that God has for us is far greater than what we go through. Romans 8:18-19 NIV says, "I consider that our present sufferings are not worth comparing with the glory that will be revealed in us. For the creation waits in eager expectation for the children of God to be revealed."

It is not easy, yes, we go through many challenges daily but if we don't give up, we will get on the other side to victory. We are the children of God, and consequently, the devil detests human beings and will not stop at anything to bring us down. By ourselves alone, we are vulnerable and weak and can become an easy target to the enemy, effortlessly overtaken. But the enemy cannot mess with us when he sees us through the blood of Jesus that was exchanged for us at the cross.

Jesus' untarnished blood paid the ultimate price for every human being, we all have been purchased from satan but we have the choice to accept or deny it. There was the wooden cross that our Messiah hung on for our sins, our abuse and brokenness because we could not have won this battle on our own without Jesus. The Bible says in Isaiah 64:6 even our best deeds are like filthy rags, we cannot get to the kingdom by being good or by doing what is good. Only through Jesus and Jesus alone, we can find redemption and acceptance.

Jesus died for our destiny on the earth and we have become His hands and feet, carrying His legacy.

I present Jesus to the world from my broken, stinking places, showing my ugly scar of molestation, of abuse and trauma of losing my child because that is where He met me, in my dark pit. God asked me to show my scar to the world so that others could see the real Jesus, who was beaten hardheartedly, who was spat on and ridiculed in public, whose clothes were stripped off his body, whose blood-spattered flesh hung out of his frames, the innocent beloved son of God who died for our sins. From His gaping wound, His precious blood was released on the ground drop by drop flowing to you and me, cleansing us from our sins. Jesus did not come to sit in holy meetings with rich leaders; He came to hang out with the sinners, the tax collectors, the outcasts, the ones whose names don't make it to important religious meetings and to the reserved seats in churches. I am hoping that this book will bring you closer to Jesus so that in His scar you can see your own.

Only by the Blood of Jesus and the word of our testimony, we can reach out to others who are hurting because like you and me, they also feel invisible and hopeless not knowing where to find solace. Don't be ashamed of your testimony because it conveys hope to another heart who might feel like they are drowning in their troubles. Scars from our past hurts and rejections validates to the world that Jesus is the healer and restorer who transformed our lives. There are many who gave their lives for the gospel of Christ. What is your testimony today? Where did the blood of Jesus find you? For many years I was burdened by my shame and insecurities, people were quick to judge me and blame me for something that others had done to me but like this lady with the Alabaster Jar, I too found grace and mercy in Gods sight. When Jesus' gaze beheld mine; He looked through me as if I was a crystal-clear glass. He observed my past, present, and my future, and looked beyond people's analytical eyes and in His eyes, I witnessed love, a kind of love that makes you drown willingly.

God in His word has pronounced that He has set before us a door that is open to anyone, the raped, the molested, the sick, the blind and the prostitute lady who was marginalized, discarded and humiliated. Forgiveness is available to anyone anytime; there are no selection criteria and no time limit.

Paying attention to well-wishers who think they are experts about our situation and give us advice from their own unfulfilled life, prevents us from chasing after our vision because sometimes we are more concerned about what others say than what God has said. People's words and deeds may hurt us but pay no heed to them for God has cautioned us (see Isaiah 54), that there is no weapon that has been built to harm us, and every tongue that dares to rise against us in judgment we would be able to condemn and bring down. This is our legacy from God who says our righteousness is of Him. We cannot earn it by our good deeds or buy it with all our riches; it is simply given to us as a gift from God.

This loose charactered woman with the Alabaster Jar did not allow gossip or rumor about her lifestyle to halt her cause to find redemption. Men lusted after her and saw her as an easy woman who they could secretly visit with their sexual fantasies while women despised her and tagged her as an evil woman, a threat to their marriage. Jesus saw a woman with many sins but beyond that, He also saw her loneliness, her longing for love and acceptance, a hope for alteration of her ways and He forgave her. She saw in Jesus a man whose kindness and mercies were infinite without recompense, who did not interrogate or exploit her. In her eyes, He saw her yearning to be loved the way she was designed to be loved and Jesus the author and finisher of all things gave her love that reserved no record of her transgressions.

Have you ever felt like an outsider, overlooked, not being able to find anyone or anything that apprehended you, searched in material benefits for that one thing that could give you a purpose, fulfill that longing in your heart, but could not find it in anything? What we search for is not on the outside, it has always been on the inside of us. That is why nothing truly satisfies us, no matter how much we have, we always strive for more, even for the wealthiest there is never enough. We don't feel complete without Jesus. He alone can truly fill that void in us that was created at the garden of Eden when human gave up their rightful inheritance to satan (see Genesis).

Acceptance and redemption are available today

This lady found Jesus and desired to be in His orbit because He *saw* her. He did not see just the external; He saw much more than the stain life choices had placed on her. He saw her brokenness, her penitence, her love, her tears and her willingness to change. Her gratitude to be accepted by Jesus was astounding. This story calls us all to break our own alabaster of shame, pain, silent suffering and rejection we have had to endure, label draped on us by people, marriage problems and everything that robs us daily, at the feet of Jesus as an act of worship. He has removed the blanket of shame from us and covered us with His own righteousness; therefore, we can walk boldly in confidence with our head held high in a room full of people because His spirit is always with us accompanying us.

His commitment to us has no strings attached. He is calling us to come to Him as we are, with all our sins. We don't have to worry about our past mistakes thinking He would accept us if we please Him by being good, because He already has. All we have to do is to receive His gift of life freely and announce it over ourselves.

Because God accepted us while we were still in sin, it is important to start declaring healing while we are still sick, *before* the disease leaves our body because Jesus Word was already sent to heal us. We can declare His word over our lives where we are, in our mess right now, and as we walk toward Jesus in faith, all those insecurities and whispers of the past must fall off us. He honors our faith and every mountain and obstacle that has been standing on our way must subside, all our dead promises and dreams are obligated to come to life because that is His promise to us, our inheritance in Him. He calls us to speak to the dry dead things in our life, dreams and hopes we gave up on because someone raped us, molested us, violated our bodies, taken away our rights and dignity. Like this woman, perhaps you too had dreams and career goals that had died because life has a way of tossing us carelessly to a corner where we are forced to make decisions that aren't Gods best for our lives. But Jesus gives us a second chance as He did to this lady with a past. When we partner with Jesus, the storms that have been tossing us from side to side must cease, the mountain before us must crumble down because our steps are ordered by the Lord, we don't just walk anywhere, meet anyone and go anywhere; He commands our steps when we trust in Him. My battered life seemed like a dead-end road; I could not get out of domestic violence despite various attempts to escape. In order to get out of a bad situation in the physical, one must get out in the mental and my head was a mess. I was in bondage in my mindset. As I nursed the painful wounds inflicted over my body, broken lips and swollen bruised eyes, my priorities were my little babies who depended on me. At times my mobility was limited by excruciating pain from the affliction but my agony led me to Jesus who had suffered pain from His own. He came to us and we did not receive Him. I understood the price Jesus paid on the cross, because unless you have suffered a bit, and lost much, you cannot bring out the good wine, because it can only come out when pressed. When we are continuously told by the person we love, that we are useless, worthless and that no one would have us, we start to believe it because we see ourselves through their eyes. Our words mean something, they carry power to build or break. Spoken words formulate a picture in our mind and we see ourselves through the words spoken to us by others. Unless we change those words by declaring positive things, we will remain in the bondage because our tongue has the power to build or break. When we cuss, it hurts someone, but when we speak a positive and encouraging word in a timely manner, people walk away empowered, even restored and refreshed.

God has given us power in our tongue, the power of life and death (see Proverbs 18:21). Use your words to build others and yourself, be an influencer, empowering and serving people because when we do, it opens doors for our own blessing.

The hurtful words of the person we love can cut through us like a knife slicing through butter and break us a little bit more each time until we are depleted of self-esteem and confidence. Encouraging and comforting words spoken in a timely manner has the power to shift mountains, open doors and heal diseases. When Jesus paid the price for our sins and rose up from the dead, God exalted His Name to the highest (see Philippians 2:9), therefore, when we speak in the authority of His Name, every demon must flee, insecurities, depression, and anxiety must exit, every plot and plan of the enemy must dismantle and every hurt from our past must evacuate. When we call on the Name of Jesus, He hears us, even if it is only a whisper or even a thought. We are undefeated when we partner with the man who sketched outside the box doing things like sending His word to heal the Centurion's servant (see Matthew 8:5), telling the dead son of a widow to get up out of his coffin (see Luke:11) or healing on the Sabbath. Jesus set a precedence before us, that words have the power to move mountains, kill fig trees and heal diseases. When we speak, we can give life or take away life.

Like this Lady with the Alabaster Jar, our past does not matter to God because God has a way of working all things out for us. Sometimes we worry for no reason because when God intervened in our circumstances, peace invaded.

Even our mistakes and painful past have been in His plan; a divorce, loss of loved ones, drug and substance addictions, that sin you thought God would never forgive you for, He has already forgiven and removed it. Psalm 103:12 has stated that as far as the east is from the west, God has removed our sin from us. If He does not remember it, why do others bring it up, why do we allow our mind to torment us? Because He has forgiven us more, we are inclined to convey to Him an astounding worship, a demon shaking outstanding worship, a worship that breaks all chains and pushes doors open and ushers His presence into our situations.

Chapter Two
Finding yourself

Life is like a wind, it can alter direction any time without warning and its forces can uproot the toughest of us. We plan strategies, but in Gods sight they are vain. All our achievements, degrees, qualifications, and hard work were futile and all our holy acts, righteous and pompous deeds, mean nothing to God. We cannot win His favor by lighting candles or with our good acts because God has already established in His word that no eye has seen, and no ear has heard all the great things He has planned for us (see 1 Corinthians 2:9), which is not based on what we do or don't do. While we may worry and lay awake at night about our health or how we will pay our invoices, or plotting and planning our next business venture, His word hems us in all around and His hand is upon us as we lie down and when we get up. We worry for not reason because He has us in the palm of His hands. He guides our steps in the journey through the trials and challenges. It makes us stronger and a better person. It is when we lose ourselves serving others, we find our calling. We can never go wrong by serving others.

Our journey is like walking barefoot on a hot desert road full of sharp rocks and thorns, some days it is down the valley, and other days it is climbing up the mountains in the heat of the blaring sun. My early recollections have been somewhat similar, where I strode barefooted on blistering gravel road to school, picking up empty long-necked beer bottles along the way and saving them to sell; drenching my feet in cold water when I came home. Similarly, Jesus is the living water where we can quench our thirst when the world scalds us with labels and discriminations.

God elects us for His purpose way before we are born. He elected and appointed us (see John 16:16, Isaiah 61), and anointed us to bring good news to the poor, to bind up the broken-hearted and declare freedom to the captives. How do we do this? By sharing our testimonies of where God found us, how He rescued us from the brink of death, how He restored us from a mental breakdown, from substance abuse, with others who are still finding their way. When we open our heart, it frees us, the problem can no longer control us. It took me many years to break free, to be able to share my story. I had to write it down and read it over and over till the pain and the shame decreased. We can never be free as long as we allow our past to control us, to hold us hostage. The son of God has set us free, we are free, but we can still choose to stay in bondage by holding onto the hurts of the past.

A remember a song we used to sing in Sunday school that every promise in the Book (The Bible), was mine. If you receive by faith and take God at His Word, all will be well with you.

When we are pushed in the deep dark hole by those we love, we tend to think about a lot of things sitting in the dark corner because we don't know our fate. As in a movie, we can see our past life playing before our eyes. We don't know if we would ever find happiness and be loved again. After a trauma in our lives, perhaps we came close to death, lost a loved one, we often come to a realization that life is too precious, and we must no longer bargain with it. The enemy tried to take me out many times, but his attempts have been futile. As a baby, I nearly died of breathing complications, but I believe God kept me alive to do His work, sharing my testimony to every soul He sends my way. One time, my chest was compressed behind a heavy pile of building materials which fell on me as I was playing hide and seek, almost killing me, but God in His mercy sent me help just on time. An air-borne roof hit my thigh during a hurricane in Fiji when I was young trying to escape from our falling roof leaving a deep incision. I have an extensive scar even to this day to remind me of the goodness of God in my life. Subsequently, I almost drowned swallowing a considerable amount of water during my own baptism in the ocean. The enemy cannot kill what God has placed inside us. He can try but it will not prosper.

Fear will hold you hostage

When my child died, I fell into a deep depression. If God had not come for me, I would have lost my life. The divorce took another child from me and at nineteen years of age, my beloved father my hero migrated to Heaven. I had breast surgery to remove pre-cancer cells, but I did not allow the storms of life to swallow me up. There is life after the flood, no matter what we lose we can build again from the broken pieces because the creator lives inside of us. God of Abraham, Isaac, and Jacob is a good God and His mercy does not change. The door opened to the enemy when I chose to go my own way, burrowing deep fangs into me like wild sprawling weed thorns and threatened to suffocate me. He was not only my God, He has been my best friend throughout my childhood, someone I relied on, communicated to and told all my fears and secrets. He has called us His children, we can go to Him without fear and reservation.

Jesus is the best gift my parents could have given me.

The enemy of God, satan recognizes that God has positioned inside of us a legacy, a talent, and once it is activated in faith, it has the power to cause him insuperable damage and for that reason, he sends his forceful troops immediately when we are born, to terminate us. When a sheep wanders off on its own from the herd and isolates itself, it becomes an easy target to wolves and bears. But when it is in the herd, it is harder to get to it. Similarly, it is easier to destroy a little plant than a huge tree. The devil wants to destroy a young person's mind before they surround themselves with other believers and become stronger in their faith walk. When we are with other believers, we are in the herd of powerful prayer warriors and it is harder for the enemy to get to us because we are stronger together than alone. When we come to Jesus, we discover that in His Name is love, redemption, forgiveness, hope and second chances. Even when we made wrong choices that took us to a different direction far away from God, He says in Isaiah 59:1, His hand is not short that He cannot reach us even in a deep dark hole, neither is He deaf that He cannot hear us when we call Him. He hears our sigh, He sees our unshed tears, He hears our whispers and our thoughts. He loves you and me more than we can ever imagine. We cannot hide from Him, whose power is felt even in the ends of the earth. He knows when we sit down and when we arise, He sees our every miniscule thought and activity. We all take our expedition of life alone, but

God promises never to leave us in our journey. Even when I was stealing bread from my neighbor's kitchen to feed my hunger, He was there. How life's situations can put us on the street begging for food and even stealing, that's why we should not judge those who are less fortunate than us because we all are only a few pay checks away from being homeless.

This part of my journey was not only about me. I had two little children who were hiking this journey with me and as broken as I was, I struggled to be the courageous and strong mother they merited. Even though I tried to conceal my tears and my hurt and pretended to be strong for them but occasionally like a dragon's fury it would surge in squirts of rage. Many who are going through domestic violence will identify with my story because that is the loneliest time of your life when you feel helpless. No one could perceive the conflict that was in my mind. Sometimes those who are the closest to you fail to observe your emotional ache or cry for help. They were only little children and were losing their father because I had decided to leave to shield us from domestic violence. My every decision affected them who were innocently counting on me to make the right choice but how did I know if it was the right choice for us, for me? That is why many sufferers of domestic violence stay because the decision making is hard especially if you have children. I had to be the provider, the mother, and the father. My mother was a widow, who was residing overseas and was my only support. Isolated, broke and alone, a destitute, I seized God's hand and boarded on the train of my new chapter.

As I rested awake on the hard floor holding my sleeping babies on my lap, who had cried themselves to sleep on a starving stomach, death became more appealing than living. In the darkness of my life, I contemplated suicide as my only option, but each time I beheld the four innocent eyes, I knew I had to live. What do you do when every door you knock is shut and every way you turn is a dead end? For a fleeting moment, I could almost feel the rejection and loneliness of Mary, the mother of Jesus when they knocked on every door to give birth to their child and every door was shut to them. I could sense her panic as they were running out of time, the baby could arrive any moment, but no door was opening to them at such an important season of her life. I was at the crossroad of my life and there seemed to be no way ahead, no door to enter and no place to rest. I looked to the right and to the left and all my eyes could behold was wilderness and insurmountable obstacles. I glanced behind and saw the long dry road I had traveled and that seemed to be the only way, but I refused to go back. I told myself that I must keep walking, even if I had to climb the mountain and walk on the thorns in the wilderness, I had to carry my children to a better and safer place. The hardest times of our lives leave us with irreplaceable survival skills, resilience and valued lessons. I remain incredibly grateful to the people who broke me, ridiculed and rejected me because they gave me something invaluable; their provoke and interrogation threw me on my knees before God who was setting me up for greatness.

I half carried my children, narrating to them imaginary happy stories of green grassland, full of flowers, birds chirping and freedom to run around, the land of milk and honey. I had waited too long, had given up too much to go back now. I kept walking, a step at a time, weary as we were, talking and encouraging myself and my children that this transition was only temporary; that there was something big and worthwhile waiting on the other side. I was homeless with no money and no belongings other than the clothes on our back. I had finally escaped after months of planning and I was terrified of being caught and taken back, so I kept dragging my heavy feet one after the other, wounded and bleeding in my heart. My life seemed like a parched, dry and scorched land. This was my Exodus, and I could not afford the luxury of sitting too long in case what I left behind caught up with us and took us back into captivity. Tears poured down my dirty dusty face as I remembered my childhood God, the God of my mother who had been my best friend. How could I end up here like this, this was far from what I had dreamt my life would be like when I was growing up. I was smart, I excelled in class. I went to a prestigious all girls international school. I was full of big dreams, but one bad decision sent me so low, that coming up again seemed impossible. Emotions hold us back from moving forward.

Our one innocent choice can turn our life upside down or excel us to something greater.

I kept moving, pulling the children by their hand, half dragging them with encouraging words, and half-truths that it was only a few more steps then we would find rest, getting them to imagine a happy place. Imagination is a powerful tool to use when we are in a crisis. It will either sink us or keep us afloat. I recalled snippets of Bible scriptures that God had commanded a bird to bring food to Elijah sitting by the river depressed and lonely, but there was no raven or uber eats who delivered us any food and there was no manna that fell from the sky in our desert. I resisted the impulse to quit my journey and go back.

When we are facing dark days, gaze at the horizon ahead and deliberate on the promise God made to us in His word that we are the apple of His eyes. Most times when I am facing difficult situations, I still repeat that till like a fire it consumes me inside giving me the strength I need to keep moving. I have to express to myself not to look back, that everything God has for me is ahead of me. I had to discover who I really was, the real me before the abuse occurred in my life and before I was branded and discriminated. Who was I that Jesus would die for me?

I had to find the plan God had for me, this could not have been His best for my life. This was a lie, I told myself.

Emotions ties us to the past

When you don't have anything to give anyone anymore, they discard you like hot rocks. I was a liability now and no one wanted me; even your own will reject you when you are down.

We all are presented with opportunities to be a blessing in other people's lives. Sometimes we miss these chances to be a servant. I was begging for milk for my two children from strangers who did not have enough for their own children, but they opened their home and heart to me. Jesus was rejected by His own (see John 1:11-13, Luke 4:14-30), the world rejected Him, yet He keeps chasing after each one of us.

I stayed awake looking at my precious sleeping children on my lap, thinking and praying, reliving my past life. We were like refugees with no place to call home, broke and broken waiting for a verdict. With the emptiness of my soul, and my mind screaming lies from the devil, I could not help but question my decision to leave my broken home, and everything that had been painful but familiar. I deliberated on fragments of Psalm 91, because that was the only scripture of the Bible that I was familiar with and had meditated enough times and knew by heart. I told myself that the God who had transported us out would not allow us to be captured again. I recollected how God parted the ocean for the children of Israel. I recited to myself that my childhood best friend, my God would come for us as He did when I was young. He was a God who had shut the mouth of Lions (Daniel 43) and looked after Joseph even in the pit (Genesis 37), and He sent him the help that took him before the King. I imagined God sending someone to bring me out from my pit.

If you have the word of God in your heart, when you need it, it will come out. Although I had not read the

Bible in quite some time but as a child, I knew the Word and in the time of need, the Word manifested itself from the well of my heart.

Even though the world might reject us but in God, we can find shelter; He will always send provision. Even when there seems to be no way in our wasteland experience, He is our navigator and knows exactly where we are always. He is God, the beginning and the end, who witnesses the sparrow fall to the ground, He sees you. Not even a leaf falls to the ground without God knowing about it. It's hard to believe the mighty powerful awesome God notices a leaf that falls, how much more He cares about us.

I sat silently, beholding the dark night, trying hard to recollect the promises of God in the Bible from my childhood days. I encouraged myself in the Lord reminding myself of all the times He came for me when I was young, saving me from the girls in school who bullied me, helping me find my lost items, providing guava for me from the tree when no one else who climbed before me found it; I surrendered to God in the still night. Even though all this seems minor, but when we see the hand of God in everything, it becomes our praise, a powerful weapon against our enemy, satan. He kept me concealed from my abuser when I hid behind shrubs holding onto my child's mouth to muffle their cry as he looked for us in the dark of the night. Even though remembering my past brought fresh tears to my eyes, but it also encouraged me and showed me the mercy of God in my life. When I didn't know if He would turn up to rescue me, He would surprise me in ways I did not expect. I remembered His faithfulness when my child died, the loneliness I felt and the deep void in my heart that was threatening to swallow me up if God had not held my heart. I was angry with God for an extended time for taking my child, God who prophesied to love also took away something that was precious to me, but I was filled with the lies of the devil then and believed him rather than

God. But even then, when I blamed Him in my misery, God still loved and stood around me holding me in His hand and forgiving me for my blindness. I told myself that He loved me too much to leave me alone now, that He did not bring us this far to leave us to the predators.

It is amusing how much you can see in the dark. My eyes were open, and I could see my past slithering like a serpent before my eyes. My simple childhood days in my parents' home, the times when I could not wait to grow up and leave home, my moments of innocent fights with my siblings, the silly arguments, all appeared too precious and valuable now as I reminisced in the shadow of the night. Tears dropped like shiny jewels from my eyes in the dusky night as memories of my sweet childhood flooded my heart. I could hear the dog barking in the distance in my parents' home, my mum's voice calling us to wash our feet before going to bed, the gentleness of my father's voice, the strength of my mum who was forever attending to our needs and did not look after her own. My heart was so overwhelmed with the memories of my childhood that my tears turned into gentle sobs as I cupped my mouth to muffle my cry. I longed for a hug from my mum and the wisdom from my dad. I regretted the moments of my rebelliousness with them when I refused to do the dishes or wanted to run away from home because they would not let me cut my hair short or pluck my eyebrows. It all seemed too trivial now. I longed to be home with them, to see them one more time. I begged God in between sobs to tell my parents in Heaven how much I loved them and that their little girl was okay.

It was because of the strong foundation of Jesus that my parents gave me that I was able to recover from depression and anxiety and from the effects of trauma.

Betrayal can hurt but it can also free us

When our own betray us, it hurts but it also liberates us because the truth sets us free. When people who had prophesied to love and keep us till death did us part betray us by defiling our bed, by bringing home another woman, it breaks us. People made fun of me, my pain was amusing to them as if they had awards for their own exemplary lifestyle. Isn't it amusing that we can laugh at other people but omit to perceive our own issues? A woman could not feel more betrayed then watching her husband with another woman in their own bed night after night. Recreating my past in my mind provided a strange comfort in my pain that I had made the right decision to escape, as I was feeling uncertain about my decision to leave. I told myself that it wasn't God's greatest for any children to be in that kind of environment. I consoled myself that I had every reason not to return to that which broke me, but there was an element of my ability to move on that was limited by my emotions. There will always be things from our past that will try to contain and restrict us from breaking free.

I was lost in the wilderness of violence and abuse, in the lies of love and second chances. Maybe you started to believe in the lies that were alleged about you, that it was your entire fault that your child died, or it was your fault your spouse left you; you deserved to be sick because you had sin in your life, but deep down you knew better? Maybe they said that if you had tried harder, made yourself better, smarter, prettier, gave more, served more, then maybe they would have looked at you properly, or loved you or not left you. I was constantly told that it was my fault that my husband had brought in his mistress, that my baby died, that there was something wrong with me, that I was cursed. Then you hear a whisper that says, to die, to accept death, that death is easier than hearing all the chatter of the people. God showed me that Jesus defeated death and that I could also learn to live in Jesus death and resurrection.

I had forgotten how it felt, to have the warm sunshine on my face and the gentle breeze gusting on my long hair making it drift spontaneously when I was young and 'hanging out' with God on the tree or under the house, chatting to Him about all my childhood giant dreams. At eighteen I got married and was barely twenty when I believed that my life had ended for me, my dreams had died, I felt depleted. I had no joy, no peace and nowhere to go. I was acutely tangled in the vicious thorns of life's trials. The more I tried to set myself free, the deeper they dug their fangs into me. I wrestled hard, but they seized me tight, seducing me with its ruthless embrace and whispers from the past. Some choices we make in life rob us of joy, dignity, respect, and self-worth.

My rebellion had taken me far from God and I wasn't certain if God would accept me back, so I made myself believe that once I sorted my life, got everything in order, then I would return to Him, and maybe then He would forgive me. I tried to be brave on my own, reassuring myself that I could fix my life as I was the one who got myself into this mess. Sometimes our choices seem good at the time when we make them, but I soon found out the greener pastures weren't so green after all. When your own body is bruised and battered, there is little you can do for others especially when there are dependent children relying on you. I was a mess both physically and mentally.

When we are broken inside and hurting, we don't feel beautiful or smart. I hated what looked back at me in the mirror. I felt torn, naked and ashamed all the time. I felt ugly and an outcast. When we abandon what we know for what gives us momentary pleasure, we open the door to the enemy. I rebelled against my childhood God and my parents, to chase after things that I knew was not God's best for me. I was in a hurry to leave my parents' home because I thought they were too strict. On hindsight now, I could not be more imprudent, making life's biggest decision based on temporary trials and superficial desires. When we are young and foolish, we are not able to see what our parents can see, a bit like God, He protects us from ourselves, decisions we make that takes us in places we have no business being.

Years I lived in fear of many things, fear of men, fear of being alone, fear of the dark, fear of falling asleep as it gave me nightmares and vivid dreams. It was like the world had left me behind, I felt invisible to everyone and no one cared, life itself had abandoned me. Some trials come in our lives for purposes beyond our understanding and even though it hurts us, and we think we will never recover but God in His mercy retrieves every broken piece and makes his exquisite master piece for His glory.

The pit can become a holy ground

Joseph's life in the Bible in Genesis resonated with me because I too had a calling of God in my life that no one understood. His own doubted his calling and threw him in the pit. Don't be surprised when people tear you down and categorize you because of your calling. From a very young age, I traveled with the missionaries who came from overseas and remained at my parent's house for the duration of their time ministering to people in the village. When my mum unknowingly elected me to accompany them, she did not realize that the seed she was planting would produce such an extensive harvest so many years later. Your calling will make a way for you, but it will also isolate you, make you a misfit because God has put you aside for His purpose. I felt deserted and betrayed by those I thought would stand by me.

I crawled in the corner in torn bloody clothes, dirty and malodorous, hungry and thirsty, with dried blood around my mouth and forehead. Strands of my hair strewn everywhere on the bloody floor from being tossed around by my hair. My heart was like a pebble in my emaciated chest. Snippets of scriptures from my early days in the Bible would drift in my mind comforting me, as blood poured from my broken body. My little children holding me and crying with me, provided a strange consolation transitorily. The Bible said to cry out to the Lord who hears his children's cry, but I could not cry anymore as if my tear ducts had a spell of drought. I would stare into space for hours and could not see people moving around me. I was there but I wasn't there, oblivious to my surroundings. Have you ever felt unseen by people, you walked right in front of them, but they did not see you?

I was bound in emotional chains crawling in a dark smelly corner of my life. I found consolation in knowing that the Lord didn't forget Joseph in jail, and neither was He going to forget me. God had brought refugees back from the utmost corners of the earth straight to safety (see Psalms 107), and He would never leave us nor forsake us.

He is loving and kind, full of mercy who forgives our mistakes and our bad choices.

You may not see Him in your problems, but He sees you. You may not know which way to turn, and I didn't know either, but He knew right where I was, and He worked everything out for His glory in my life. In my troubles was my truth hidden. Losing myself in Him completely, forgetting who hurt me, who left me, I was able to find myself, the real me, the one who He had called me to be, the worshiper, the Kings kid. When I saw myself in His eyes, I was able to forgive others because, in His light, everything else became small and insignificant. Where He was taking me, was larger than any hurts or grudges I held in my heart. I had to let go to free myself for my greater. It may take a while to discover ourselves in the maze of life choices we make, or what others did to us, or that disease that robbed us, but God's mercy identifies us and will find us. He comes looking for us like a good

Sheppard who goes looking for that one lost sheep and when he finds it, rejoices and celebrates (see Luke 15:3-7).

Chapter Three
Comfort or Vision

When we are too relaxed and comfortable in bed or on a couch, it becomes difficult to get up even for a beverage. Being content and too comfortable can deter us from seeking our calling, from exploring new venues and opportunities. It can prevent us from stretching our imagination and visions and will often keep us stagnant in one place. Life sometimes presents us with difficult situations that can take us far away from what we hold close to our heart, from our own values and morals. Instead of fighting these challenges, we often accept them and become comfortable, even if it hurts us. To explore new horizons it requires stepping out, taking risks and trying new options. If we are too comfortable in one place, we will never leave.

Some difficult situations in life have a way of pushing us out of comfort zone. Such contests make us resilient and bring out hidden gifts that would not have come out any other way.

We take God's silence as an answer to settle for less and give in to our circumstances. Some choices we make opens the door to the enemy, and it is not God who is punishing us, but faith can pull us out of those situations, if we believe.

Faith is taking risks; it's like living on the edge, not knowing from day to day where your next meal will come from. Abraham in the Bible left his families, his friends and everything that was familiar to him to follow God and that was a risk he resolved to take. He didn't know where He was going but He knew He could trust God (see Genesis). David did not go into any battle without first seeking God's approval. Joshua took risks when his army seized the land of Canaan knowing that there were strong giants there. God honors deep-seated risk-taking faith, kind of faith that says you may be huge and powerful Goliath but guess what, I am a force to be reckoned with because I know who fights for me. Peter knew it was impossible to walk on the water, but he took a risk and stepped out of the boat onto the water at Jesus' call. Moses led a massive assembly of people out of bondage from a very powerful King by faith alone and a stick as his only weapon. God calls us all to trust Him completely without reservation or a backup plan. We go to His school of training. He uses our pain and circumstances to train and qualify us for His positions.

In some situations, we find it easier to stay than to get out because getting out means facing new unfamiliar challenges. When we rebel against everything, we hold close to our heart, including our dreams, and leave everything that mattered to us for someone we thought would love us, we often feel ashamed that it did not work out and stay in the brokenness trying to make sense of it all.

We want to prove to everyone that all was well, so we stay and pretend and make the brokenness our home, our norm, our life. Settling for less is not Gods best for our lives. Jesus did not give His life for us to settle for less.

For me finding work, a new home and someone to mind the children was terrifying. Many girls who took a risk like this ended up in prostitution. And that was one of the reasons I stayed in my situation for so long even if it was hurting me and killing me slowly inside, because it was safer than going out into the world alone and taken advantage of my vulnerability. Taking a step into the unknown can be intimidating, therefore, many stay in abusive relationships, in dead-end jobs because it is familiar.

However, God has a way of forcing us out of our comfort zone by presenting us with demanding situations where we have no choice but to surrender to Him.

Finding your sweet spot

I desired to discover my vision, the purpose God had created me for. I wanted to find out what my strength was. The Bible says in Proverbs 29:18 KJV, that without vision, people perish. Without realizing, I had been in the ministry of healing and evangelism since I was a child, sharing the gospel of Jesus Christ to the people in the community. I assumed that my vision had died when I walked away from God to live my life my own way. But we serve a God who is the resurrection and the life. A God who is merciful and for whom nothing is dead, nothing is a waste, and there is no mistake that He cannot fix and no dead thing He cannot bring to life. When we don't have a purpose, a vision in life, we will be swayed in whichever direction. As for me without a clear vision and a purpose in my life, I did not know who I was and where I was going. Like the lady with the Alabaster Jar, I needed to find out who I really was, what my calling was.

When I worked in aged care as a caregiver, I looked at the registered nurses pushing the medication trolley, assessing the patients and giving out medications, and I dreamed of becoming one. That dream became a goal when I firmly decided and took steps towards it. It was extremely hard to juggle little children and a job, but my vision was before my eyes and it pushed me to my goal. Seeing myself pushing that medication trolley, formed an image in my mind and slowly it seeped into my heart and my life. I started to *call* it out by telling everyone that I was soon to be a nurse before I even got a place at the university. I imagined it before it became real. Romans 4:17 says to call those things that be not as though they were. God told Abraham in Genesis to see the stars and imagine having that many children before it happened for him. When you write your vision down and keep it before your eyes daily and imagine it in your mind, it becomes real because you follow what you think about the most. Whatever occupies our mind the most, the body tends to follow it because that is how God made us. Our mind is the most powerful part of our body. As long as I felt small and weak, did not think I could ever get out of my situation, it kept me captive in its prison. But when I started to change my thoughts and imaginations, I started to speak positive declarations and even though I was still in the same situation, but something had shifted in me. I felt powerful and able on the inside. The right thoughts and imaginations can help us out of any situation.

The Bible says in Habakkuk 2:2, to write your vision, make it plain on tablets; keep it before your eyes, look at it, ponder on it, believe it until it became a reality. See a happy place in your mind and your heart, a haven where you can find relief.

The lady with the Alabaster Jar had a clear vision in her heart. She knew she wanted to see Jesus and to ask for His mercy and she acted toward achieving her goal regardless of how difficult the task was, getting past her accusers and all those who called her names. Without a purpose in life, we will easily be persuaded and influenced by those around us to do things they want us to do. That is why some of us fall into doing things that get us in trouble.

Even when we are in a bad situation, the Bible pronounces that if we see ourselves getting out of it in our mind, our actions will follow. Vision in our minds forms a photograph and in time it converts into reality. If we desire the comfort of a laid-back life, then we will miss on our purpose because only radical people who chase after their dream make it. When we live by faith, it is knowing from day to day that He is the one who supplies our daily bread because God says to live by faith in total submission to Him, trusting Him for everything. He says in Matthew 4: 4 NIV, "Man shall not live on bread alone, but on every word that comes from the mouth of God," He wants us to trust

Him for everything in our lives, to put Him first and foremost.

We are all called to be His hands and feet, to minister the gospel of Christ, to lay our hands on the sick and when we recognize that He is not looking for the perfect but anyone who is willing, we have a kind of confidence that is different from other people. All the attacks from the enemy cannot stop His purpose from manifesting in our lives. We feel a sense of peace because we know who has our back. The Bible says our gifts and talents (see Proverbs 18:16), will bring us before great people, and open doors so that our gifts can bring God glory. When we start using our gifts and talents wherever we are, it opens doors for more. No one knows everything, but once we start where we are with what we have, God will reveal to us the next step. We just have to begin by faith and take that first step.

Showing your scar to those who are coming from behind

When we share our testimonies of where the Blood found us with people, it helps them to see the real Jesus in us. When we allow others to see our broken pieces, the attempts we have made to leave our situations to start a new life but like an addiction to a drug, we kept returning to what broke us till God's mercy found us, it acts as a balm to their bruises. They are able to perceive the grace of God in our testimonies and find reassurance in knowing that the same God who saved us can save them too. There are a lot of suffering and hurting people who need to hear your heart speak from your broken places, from the place of your addictions and strongholds, from where you could not depart without Jesus' help. Don't hide your light. Shine it so that others can find their way out from their dark places.

The word of God says that darkness and light cannot work together. Where there is light, the darkness must dispel. God and sin cannot live together. When God arrived in our life, every stronghold had to exit; strongholds we might have allowed by way of choices that took root and kept us chained; it could have been toxic relationships, bitterness and addictions to things that preoccupied our minds and our hearts and keep us away from Gods presence. The Word of God says that the Blood of Jesus broke every stronghold of satan in our lives, so why do we choose to chain ourselves to things that are harmful to us? Unforgiveness keeps us chained to our past. Just because someone did something horrible to us does not make us a bad person. What happened to me did not define me. Even though the memories of it haunted me for years and fear and anxiety penetrated my every movement keeping me in shackles, I wrestled against it before it could cage me in. My fears had trapped me in the past that someone would sneak into my room and violate me or my children. Even though after a trauma we try to move on but some things like a pendulum hangs over us reminding us that we are tainted, tarnished and not good enough for the master's table.

I had a choice; either to remain a victim or to use my brokenness as a blueprint to my destiny, regardless of what others said, a highway to my purpose and abundant life. I refused to allow the latter to control my present. God did not forsake me even in the slumps of my life and He will also not abandon you.

Our choices take us through a detour to God, but the word of God says He is never late. He has a way of accelerating us for all the time lost.

God wants us to live the best life He gave us, to dream big and trust in His love. His blessing is not just for us, it is a generational blessing that will outlive us.

Today I praise God that those challenges in life made me a strong, confident and compassionate person. That which God has placed inside of us comes out when we are pressed or pushed to a corner because only in the dark, a seed is able to sprout. Your pain and your mess were all in His will, and He will bring it all to a good purpose. I can laugh now and say that my beautiful virtuous mum who never wasted anything, she could turn the leftover food into something tasty, God also does not allow anything to waste. I did not know at the time that the pain and the anguish I had yielded to, the terrifying moments of my life was going to become somebody's strength someday, a testimony that would touch lives.

I did not allow the challenges and abuse to frame the outline of my life. I used it to make me a worshipper, the one who drew strength from the past and used the tears to quench her thirst. When the drops of my tears touched His feet, His hand reached out and lifted me up. His robe of righteousness covered my torn body. When God touches your heart and brings you healing and restoration, you will no longer follow the things of the past. He has a way of making all things new and uses your experiences to bring you closer to your calling.

The greater the calling, the more the devil is threatened and will send his army to pull us down and distract us from our cause. The calling of God on our life warrants us the front row seat into the enemy's hit list. We get attacked more than other people. If you are wondering why you always have issues, your car breaks down, your washing machine gives up, people talk about you, pull you down, pain in your body, nothing happens right, know that your name is in the most wanted list of satan, but your worship is your weapon in this warfare you are in. Worship will drown the enemy in our lives.

They might have gotten away with putting us in the prison of despair or designing the label of reoffender, or prostitute, homeless, orphan or whatever they have called us, that reputation does not matter to God. They also put the label of 'guilty' on Jesus too. He became guilty, who was without sin, for you and me.

Calling ushers trouble

Calling comes at a very high price just as Jesus' calling cost Him His life. He came for one purpose, to die in our place. The Bible narrates that other people had callings that cost them something of value. Joseph was the first son born to Jacob through his beloved Rachel. Jacob loved Rachel more than any of his other wives, but she could not have children for a long time. Therefore, Jacob enjoyed having Joseph close to him and loved him much since he had him in his senior years. But God had a heavenly purpose for this young boy. The story of Joseph extents to many chapters in the book of Genesis whose own siblings wanted to harm him because they were jealous of him, that their father favored Joseph and had made him a coat of many colors. The reflection of this narrative is that his brothers hated him because when Joseph was around them, they could not do corrupt and evil activities because Joseph was honest and transparent, and he told his father everything he had witnessed his brothers' do. They must have detested him with a passion to want to slay him. They resolved their planning by throwing him in the pit, then narrated a lie to their elderly father that the animals had killed Joseph. The devil will use those closest to you to betray and hurt you the most. Moses' own siblings spoke negatively about his calling and brought punishment on themselves. Be careful whom you judge, you don't want what happened to Moses' sister happen to you. Joseph's and Moses's siblings did not recognize that nothing they could do or say could halt Gods plan. Each of our calling is different. Whoever God designates for His work is His business. His purpose for each one of us is different. When can only be our best when we are walking in our own purpose, and not wearing someone else's armour?

Joseph's calling that was in his life came with a cost; his own siblings hated him, and he spent twelve long years of in prison. Joseph's calling could not be shut down, neither could it be aborted. Even in the prison cell, Joseph's calling was overflowing because what God has given you, will start to demonstrate wherever you are. You will not be able to contain it.

No plotting and planning of the enemies of Joseph could edge him in, even behind the prison doors he began his ministry to the cellmates by interpreting their dreams and serving them. You might have served time, and suffered loss, but that does not obliterate your calling. In Romans 11:29, it says that our calling is irrevocable.

God's word comes with a lifetime warranty with no strings attached. Gifts are not a reflection of integrity. We are all called for a purpose, each one of us, and although we may run, hide, rebel and get involved in other passions, we cannot hide from God and His love. Your calling will find you, it will start to spill out of you like an overflowing cup. What God has given to you is yours for keeps. God does not change His mind about you. No one can take it from you, they may imitate you, copy you, walk and dress like you, but no one can be you. You are one of a kind, fearfully and wonderfully made, there is no one exactly like you in the world, (see Psalm 139:14).

God chose you before you were conceived in your mother's womb and before anyone could put a label on you, before you had a chance to make choices. You were not a mistake and did not just burst upon earth unannounced. You were called into being by God. You were destined to be born at this time, in this era, because God has a job for you that only you can do. You have a reserved seat with your name on it. Way before you were born, it was already set aside, no matter what you do, where you run to, the calling of God in your life and His love will draw you to Him like a kite being pulled by its master. Our mistakes have been our training ground, as God uses every situation in our lives to prepare us for His purpose and for His glory. When the heat and storm of life take its toll on us, God says He leads us beside still waters and restores our soul (see Psalm 23). He beckons us to walk with Him to still waters, where we can find peace and serenity from the stressors of life. He is the living water in our life that restores our souls and brings us peace, strength and freshness.

Bible says in Psalm 130:13 ESV, "For you formed my inward parts; you knitted me together in my mother's womb. I praise you, for I am fearfully and wonderfully made." You are special, made in the very image of God for His purpose. You have a vision growing inside of you like that of a pregnant woman, ready to burst out of the seed. Whatever your calling is, be it teaching, cooking, preaching, business, craft, welding, carpentry, do it like you are doing it unto God and He will bless the work of your hands. And in everything, give Him Glory for without His grace, we would not be here. Do you know how many incidences and accidents He saves us from every day? We have a blood mark of Jesus on us and the devil cannot touch us without Gods permission. And anyone who must take permission is not the Master. In Exodus, the death angel passed by every house that had the blood on the door post.

It is not by chance that you are reading this book. If you walk away with whatever revelation He is showing you in this book, your life will never be the same again. By faith, we believe and by faith, we have received.

The price of calling is costly

There is a cost to everything good. Every great man and woman of God in the Bible paid a price for their calling. My calling made me a loner. I never fitted in anywhere and always felt like I did not belong. I was on my prayer walk one day, feeling overwhelmed about everything I believed God had placed in my heart to do, asking God to send me help, I heard in my spirit, "Eagles fly alone." I didn't know what He meant by that till I went home and did a research about Eagles and found out they were solitary creatures with great confidence in themselves like a true leader. They were not afraid of storms, in fact, they used the storm to propel them to fly higher.

As long as you are accepted by God, it does not matter who reject you, who is for you or against you. If you lose your family to follow God, God will give you many families because your calling is not for you. It is to bring Him glory and not to make everyone happy.

Moses who grew up in the palace with the best of education and material things, found himself a misfit, not Hebrew enough and not Egyptian enough. Calling of God in your life will make you feel like you did not belong anywhere, you will feel like a loner, not fitting anywhere and no one understanding you. He meandered in the desert alone and depressed till the time came for God to bring him back to his calling that He had been training him for since his birth. I was afraid of driving in busy cities and one day I was placed in a big city in the peak hour traffic and I had no choice but to drive in fear, but each moment it was setting me free. You can feel the fear but do it anyway showing the devil that nothing can hold you back from God. God will sometimes take you back to face the giants you were afraid of once. God is the father who knows His children the best. He would never allow your foot to be moved. He said in Psalm 121:3 NIV, "He will not let your foot slip; He who keeps you will not slumber."

God does not ignore our prayers. No, it does not end up in His junk mail collecting dust. What He has called us to be will manifest in our lives. Mary, the mother of Jesus gave up her own dreams and desires in submission to God's calling for her life. Abraham and Sarah both had yearned for a child as Sarah was barren and God blessed them with a child in the senior years of their life. Hannah was tormented and oppressed by her husband's other wife for not having a child until it was time for God to open her womb and she conceived Samuel, who she presented back to God in worship. It is never too late for God. The doctors had pronounced a diagnosis of possible breast cancer on me, I prayed to God and even though I had to go through procedures, but He healed me; whatever is your cry to God, He hears you. We may feel pain in our bodies, perhaps when we look around, all we see is lack in our lives, but for God, none of those things matter. He can make something out of nothing. He does not need a reason to bless you.

Ecclesiastes 3:2 narrates that everything has a time and a purpose on earth. In due season He will restore you, your calling will manifest because what God starts, He completes. He sees the end from the beginning, and He is true to His Word. All we have to do is to continue to give Him glory as we wait for the manifestation on earth what has been already ordered in Heaven. Waiting is hard but it is not the time to fold our hands and sit on the relaxing chair. Waiting means trusting God in our downtime and preparing for our harvest; a time of worship and meditation on His promise and giving Him glory while we declare things into being. We also believe and get organized for His blessing just as a farmer who plants seeds after careful preparation of the soil and then he gets ready for harvest. He starts his search for the harvesters, gets the barn ready and plans his harvest. Likewise, when we pray, believe you receive it and get ready for the breakthrough.

Worship is intimacy with God

It costs to worship like this lady with the Alabaster Jar, laying it all before God, all our heart, secrets, our whole being, holding nothing back. Worship is a sacrifice of our self even when there is a fight going on inside us between our flesh and our spirit. When we continue to worship despite our external circumstances and our internal turmoil, our spirit rises alert and ready to do the will of God.

We search all our lives for that one object that makes us feel alive and complete, and we look for it in the material things, in the jobs and high-profile positions and in people and relationships, in drugs and alcohol and in money and fame, but God hid it in the inside of us. The devil knows that God has put inside of us a seed that has the power to change the world. Our worship hails God in our situation and when God arrives, satan must leave. If you have been wondering why you are always having troubles in your life even though you are living a Godly life, it is because you became an enemy to satan when you accepted Jesus as your Lord and savior. It is not about you; His battle is with God. God desires to love us, and the devil wants to control us. satan is not happy that God made us just a little lower than the angels and calls us his children and gave us our own Kingdom, the earth.

If he can destroy us early in life with worries, confuse our identity with low self-esteem, fear, and self-condemnation, and then he knows we will not be able to walk in our calling. That is why satan is after our minds and thoughts because if he can cause chaos in our minds, he has us confused and in doubt. But like the lady at Jesus' feet, we too can find healing, redemption, acceptance, and hope. It does not matter how deep in sin you are in, if you are reading this in the jail cell, remember Joseph was in the jail and God used him there as well. He did not give up hope and continued to do what is right even in the jail and God lifted him up and out. The name of Jesus has power beyond our understanding and when we call on that name, the Word of God says He hears us and comes to rescue us. His name has the power to scoop us out of bad situations. In the night when Paul and Silas sang hymns and praised

Him in the jail, it shook and broke the very chains and opened the doors (see Acts 16:25-26).

In the book of Acts 12:6-8, it is narrated that Peter was tied with two chains and as he slept between two guards while another guard was on duty at the prison gates, and in the midnight hour an angel of the Lord suddenly appeared and woke him up. He told Peter to put his shoes and his robes on and escorted him out of the prison. God is so merciful that He cares even about our comfort, directing Peter to put his shoes and cloak on, that is how loving a father God is. God cared about the children of Israel when they demanded meat in the desert, and He sent them quails to satisfy their hunger as narrated in the book of Exodus. God is not what religion has taught us for a long time, someone who punishes us every time we open our mouth or do the wrong thing by Him. His love is ceaseless, persistently forgiving us and His mercy is forever. He cares even about how we feel. God asks Cain in Genesis 4:6 why his countenance was down even though He knew everything about Cain, yet He cared enough to ask Cain why he was upset, what was bothering him. In 1 Kings 19:7, we can see how caring God is when He wakes Elijah up twice, to give him food and water, telling him to rest in preparation for a long journey ahead. God's love is abounding and forever looking out for us.

Bad things will happen, and we will make wrong choices and decision that will take us far away from God, but God says in Isaiah 59:1 NIV, "Surely the arm of the LORD is not too short to save, nor his ear too dull to hear."

He is never too far away from us even when we may have drifted away from Him and lost our way back home. He even hears our sigh and our unshed tears and sends us help.

Confine those thoughts that tell you that you are not good enough and abort those voices of guilt in your mind telling you that your sins are too many and too bad for God to forgive. You may have started out in a depraved place, but you don't have to stay there. The beginning does not matter; it is how we end up that matters. Some of our beginning might hold bad memories for us, but you can use that pain to propel you to your destiny. Tell your story, as it may speak in other people's lives, because when we serve others and influence others who are struggling in their journey, it allows healing in our own lives and opens doors for our blessing. There is someone out there who will be encouraged from your story.

He hears those who call on His name, His ear is always listening to His children, like a parent even though we may be busy in the home, our ears are always open to the cries of our children. I was in a place of impossibility and feeling disheartened about my choices, had given up all hope of ever getting out, when God moved mightily and rescued me. I too believed the lies of satan thinking I was never going to amount to anything and that my mess was just too big and too hard even for God to fix. It was lies, and the devil is the master of lies. When we pay attention to him, we give him power and make him important. When we call on the name of Jesus, regardless of where we are, even in a dark place, He will hear us and save us (see Romans 10:13).

Not allowing others to come in the way of your destiny

In the Bible in Luke 18:35, is this sweet story of a blind man sitting begging when he overheard that Jesus of Nazareth was passing by. He did not want his debility to get in the way of his opportunity. He had no one to escort him to Jesus, but that too did not distress him. He had no vision, but he used his voice and started calling on top of his voice the Name of Jesus. Even when people expressed to him to be silent, the Bible says, he continued to shout till he caught Jesus' attention. Jesus hears our sigh, He sees our unshed tears, hears our whispers and our thoughts and loves us more than we can ever imagine. Like this blind man, when we cannot go to Jesus, Jesus comes to us. Sarah laughed to herself when she thought of having a child in her old age with her old impotent husband, but the Lord heard her laughter even though she had not laughed on the outside (see Genesis 18:12-15). God hears us when our heart is full of sorrow and we are not able to pray, we may not outwardly be able to utter a word. Your heart may be overwhelmed right now, and you don't know what to articulate to God, God knows your heart and reads your tears.

We all take our journey alone and must walk the path set out for us, but God promises never to leave us. We all make mistakes, and although some mistakes take us far away from our values, our loved ones and from God. and although people may discard us as a lost cause and say that nothing good could become of us, God sees something far greater and precious in us. People label us for all sorts of reasons, sometimes because of our stature, how thin or big we are, or our profession, what we may do for a living; they categorized this lady with the Alabaster Jar as sinful after witnessing her engaging in the act of adultery, but Jesus forgave her also, no questions asked. People would be quick to judge you, call you names, laugh and ridicule you while they cover their own sinful lives. We make conversation about people behind their back, but when others do the same about us, it hurts us, we block them, we don't want to talk to them, we tell others how much they have hurt us, yet when we do the same, somehow, we believe it is okay. Before we talk about others, Jesus calls us to look at our own sin.

"Why do you look at the speck of sawdust in your brother's eye and pay no attention to the plank in your own eye? How can you say to your brother, 'Let me take the speck out of your eye,' when all the time there is a plank in your own eye? You hypocrite first take the plank out of your own eye, and then you will see clearly to remove the speck from your brother's eye," Matthew 7:3-5 NIV.

In Joshua 2, there was a lady called Rahab who was a well-known prostitute, but God still used her in His extensive strategy. Before we judge others, we don't know God's plan for their lives. Zacchaeus was an ill-reputed tax collector who also happened to be of short stature, (see Luke 19:1-10*)*, found out who he really was when Jesus interjected his life by inviting himself to Zacchaeus' house for dinner. Zacchaeus was not popular; people did not like him because of his profession. He very likely had low self-esteem because he was different from other people, he was a short guy and his job alienated him from others. He must have felt lonely, perhaps had no friends and had his own issues he was dealing with when Jesus overlooking the other hundreds of people flocking him, distinguishes this little guy up a tree because Jesus saw what others did not see. When we are laden heavy with issues of life to a breaking point and no one understands us, we have no one to confide our heart to, Jesus understands and hears our hearts even when we are not able to formulate a coherent speech to Him in prayer.

One day I was walking with a friend when I slipped and fell on a huge slimy rock on the beach, landing on my side hitting the rock hard and cracking my ribs in the process. As I passed out in agony, I could only 'think' the Name of Jesus. The pain was so excruciating that inhaling and exhaling were impossible, let alone speaking. Because of my relationship with God since my childhood, at that time, automatically I would have prayed but all I could do was to think the Name of Jesus before everything became black. When I woke up there were all these people around me telling me the ambulance was on its way and to stay still, but Jesus had heard my 'thought' and in His Name alone is the power to heal. I was totally healed, able to inhale and exhale without any pain or complications. Even when I was not able to call out or even pray because of such pain, 'thinking His Name Jesus' was ample.

In the breaking is your making

Sometimes God will leave us in our mess because the lessons we acquire in our mistakes and our wrong choices, we cannot learn any other way. The people who hurt me did more for me than those who said they loved me. By pressing me they were actually bringing out Gods purpose in me. If it wasn't for my breaking, I would not have my testimony and this book. My dark solitude place revealed who my friends and my foes were. Troubles have a way of sieving our friends. Those we thought would be there for us surprise us by being the first to leave us. When Jesus went to the Mount Gethsemane to pray, His friends, the ones who shared meals with Him could not feel His pain (see Luke 22:39-46). Very few people will be willing to share your pain, sit there with you night and day as long as it takes, pray for you and be there for support without asking for anything in return but there are some who are like parasite, as long as they get something out of a relationship, they are in it, but as soon as there is nothing for them, they will leave for the next kill. Be aware of those people in our lives who will only do things if there was something in it for them to gain. They call it working both ways, give and take. Jesus did not give and take. He just gave. We have received freely, we also give freely, be a servant, always look out for ways to make a change in people's lives, especially those who are not able to return our favour.

Sometimes people in our life cannot handle what God has for us and they leave. Let them depart because all our paths cross for reasons. Your weeping and your grief were positioning you to the place to receive from God. God has said that our weeping may endure for the night, but joy will come in the morning (see Psalm 30:5). God is getting ready to set a table for you in front of your adversaries, the ones who discredited and humiliated you will see you in a place like Joseph where you will be able to bless them. Keep your peace when they mock you and shame you because God has said, "Do not be deceived, God is not mocked, for whatever one sows, that will he also reap," (Galatians 6:7 ESV).

Sometimes people don't like us without a cause. They don't even know why they don't like us. It is because they see something in us that they cannot comprehend, and when people cannot understand something and cannot work us out, they dislike us, reject us, put us away. Something about us, whispers truth into their darkness. The word of God in us is a mirror to them. They see something they cannot explain, and it disturbs them, so they pull you down or ignore you because they cannot handle your light.

We are the light in their darkness and light exposes the truth and truth sets us free. No person pulls down another who is in a lower place than themselves. They will always pull down someone who is at a higher level than them because they cannot go any higher themselves, so they must pull us down to be in the same level as them to make them feel good. Shine the brightest wherever you are, in whatever position God may have placed you.

Removing the mask takes courage

Sometimes we go about our everyday life hiding behind a mask of false claims, telling ourselves that all is well in our life, that we have it all together, but the reality may be something else. God sees our shattered spirits; our hushed tears and He will re-establish us when we are prepared to lay down our disguises at His feet. We are never unaccompanied and never out of grasp to God.

In Jeremiah 1:5 GNT, God has said that He had already spoken about you before you were born, "I chose you before I gave your life and before you were born, I selected you to be a prophet to the nations." Remove the mask and embrace yourself, with all your flaws and all your mistakes, let God heal your broken wings as you spread them out to fly. Fall in love with yourself because you are your own best supporter.

Alone in the wilderness running away from his past, depressed, lonely and confused about whom he was, God met with Moses in the burning bush. Maybe you also have been running away from something, but it seems to catch up with you. I was running away from my calling, even when I left the country and changed states, He still found me. Where can we hide from God, the Psalmist articulates that God is everywhere (see Psalm 139), we cannot flee from His spirit, He knows every move we make, He knew where Jonah was (see Jonah). The Bible in 1 Samuel *3* has described that God called Samuel three times. Even when we don't hear God calling us, He will call us repeatedly till we hear His voice behind us. Don't feel that you have somehow missed your chance, because He will call you repeatedly till you submit to Him.

We can hide behind a facade and pretend that everything was great for us but silently we battle with poor self-image and self-worth, seeing ourselves as lowly and unworthy to be loved. God has called you to be extraordinary.

Low self-esteem is how we see and perceive ourselves. It wasn't so much about what other people thought or whispered about me, it was my own perception of myself that kept me isolated and in the jail of depression. I saw myself as weak, timid, and helpless. I had a lot of 'poor me' thoughts that I needed to destroy. It was a distorted image of how God saw me. The Bible says in Numbers 13:33 KJV, the children of Israel saw themselves weak as grasshoppers in front of giants; "And there we saw giants, the sons of Anak, which come of the giants and we were in our own sight as grasshoppers." The neighbors and the enemies of the children of Israel feared and revered them, as they were the dominating kingdom, arrayed in influence and were under the shield of God. Their status of deposing the most powerful army of Egypt had spread like wildfire to all the neighboring towns. Every household gossiped about how God had parted the red sea for them but one thing they did not know was that in their own sight, the children of Israel fell short. They doubted their ability to be anything but slaves.

On the other hand, we see David who was only a young boy when God called him, and he saw himself as a strong warrior in front of a giant. David did not acknowledge Goliath as someone he needed to be fearful of, unlike the public who saw him as a powerful giant. David called him, "This uncircumcised Philistine", who he declared to slaughter just as he had the lions and bears in his job. David did not see himself as an untrained soldier, but rather a strong experienced fighter. David was very certain that he would win the battle. He made a public announcement before he went into battle, "This day the LORD will deliver you into my hands, and I'll strike you down and cut off your head (1 Samuel 17, NIV).

His vision was bigger than himself. He saw himself as a definite winner in the battle that was ahead of him. He did not have much in his hands to fight with, but He knew who was going with him in the battle. How did a young boy find such strength, courage, and confidence to challenge a huge powerful, fearful giant that even the most skilled armed forces could not take down? This was not the first time he was coming against something that stood in the way of his calling. He knew that the same God who gave him countless victories with his opponents in his job as a caretaker of sheep, had not changed and was going to give him success with the giant regardless of its size. David had already won the battle in his mind, and if you win in the mind, you win in the physical. He was an experienced passionate fighter, and had gained many victories previously, which made him certain about his success in this battle, because he compared the giant with his past rivals who were no match to him. First, he won in his mind, he saw an image of himself bringing down his opponent and then he expressed his victory by faith with his mouth. When I had to go through the surgery to remove pre-cancer cells from my breast, it was the fear I was fighting in my mind. Physical pain was bearable, it was the mind I had difficulty taking control of. How many nights we lie in bed unable to sleep because of that one niggling thought that might sneak in our mind like a snake and take our joy and peace away. It really does not matter how much we preach about faith, or listen to faith sermons, we all fight demons in our mind. It is a constant battle. David here very nicely demonstrates how to use vision in your mind and speak or prophesy by faith what you are trying to achieve. He saw in his mind and spoke it out with his mouth. Abraham did the same, he saw in his mind being a father of many nations and he spoke it out by calling himself the father of many nations. Write your vision down, see the image in your mind and speak it out. It does not take long for the mind and the mouth to get in alignment for your project to materialise.

Often, we believe what other people say about us, how we should look and feel rather than what God has said about us. Once we discard the false pretense and accept ourselves just the way we are as Jesus sees us, we will have peace and joy in all that God has called us to do in Him.

Our low self-esteem derives from hurts from our past, something traumatic that has happened to us. Sometimes it can be a sickness or a disease that leaves us with a label, separates and isolates us from people. We lose hope, give up on our dreams and cease to fight. We accept our bad situation and become despondent.

Here is a story of four men who found themselves in a bad situation and instead of giving up and accepting their fate which appeared grim and dismal; they wrestled with their circumstances till they came up with a conclusion. After cautiously reviewing all their options, they collectively came up with a strategy. Although it had risks that could have killed them, they opted to take the bold perilous step which pushed them to a new dimension. Sometimes in our own lives, we become trapped in a corner and may not have a lot of options available to us. Whichever direction we choose has traps and obstructions, but we cannot stay where we are. Rather than accepting their hopeless situation, staying where they were, and giving up altogether, because of the impossible situation in their lives, they decided to move rather than stay stagnant, even if they met up with death.

In 2 Kings, Chapter 7, we read of these four men who suffered from a dreaded skin disease. Deprived of further medical investigation and sympathy, they were thrown out of the town. Their skin disease was perceived to be transmittable and fatal. As a result, these four men were isolated, rejected and discarded from the community they grew up in. When people cannot understand your condition or your sickness, they will abandon you and put you away, or discard you as a lost cause. Many times, the government categorizes and labels people, gives them money and put them away. These men did not do anything wrong, they did not break the law, they did not commit a crime, they were flung out of their homes and the city because they were sick. They had no control over their disease, it was not their fault. They did not do anything to bring it upon themselves, it just originated. Sometimes in our lives, we may be going our own merry way, and something bad occurs that diverts the course of our lives. An accident or an incident that cripples our body and perhaps leaves us on a wheelchair for the rest of our lives, or a broken heart that is reluctant to heal, or maybe a diagnosis of a terminal illness that can leave us alone and feeling hopeless.

The Bible enunciates that these men parked themselves outside the city gates, stranded, unaided and feeling unloved. Not only were these four men ailing with a disease, but they had lost their homes, their occupations and income, rejected by their own families and from everything that they held close to their heart. They had no money, not that anyone would have traded with them. They had no belongings and no possessions. With no fault of their own, they had unexpectedly lost everything and walked away with nothing.

Fighting demons in your head

Sometimes all we want is to hear a gentle word or someone to hold us and love us for who we are, not because of what we have or what they can obtain from us. When we go through threatening periods or lose our health, material things cease to matter. In the Bible, are many people who had everything, vast agricultural empire, servants, silver and gold, but desired for one thing that they could not have. Abraham was extremely well-off but could not have any children to leave his assets to. Naaman in 2 Kings was a man of high ranking, a chief commander of the army who socialized with the governors and sat down with Kings and senators, but he had a secret. He struggled to conceal the foul smell of rotting flesh under his clothes from his illness. All his power and wealth could not give him health. Jairus in Luke 8:40 was a famous leader of a mega church, but He was not able to activate his faith for his dying daughter.

David was an influential King of fabulous wealth and a worshipper after Gods' own heart, yet all his power, fame and wealth could not save his dying child. Material things may look great on the outside and even provide us with momentary pleasure, but when our health or our loved one's health is compromised, all the empire we have fashioned cannot help us. Like salt, it soon loses its flavor and becomes worthless.

These four men, forlorn and homeless like vagabonds, sitting outside of what was once their home, also had properties that were significant to them, but when they became unwell, they were disposed of swiftly by their families and everyone they affiliated with. Their assets could not save them. We could go to work one day and not return home or go to the doctor for slight pain and return with a terminal diagnosis. A poor woman sits on the floor of her humble home with her husband and children, and they break their bread together with laughter and joy of intimacy, but secretly longing in her heart for a nice home, a dining table and a nice meal while the rich lady sits alone in her long elaborate dining table in her huge mansion wishing that her husband and children were home with her having a meal. We don't know what we have till we don't have it anymore. The poor lady had her family around her having their simple meal in their squalor home, while the rich lady was eating alone in her lavish home. Rich or poor, we all have something we are struggling with, be it sickness, loneliness, relationship issues, financial issues, debts, hopelessness, or poverty, we all must carry our cross on us. These men sat there hungry, cold and alone, each in their own profound thought.

Have you ever been rejected and despised by your own and had to walk away with nothing but the clothes on your back? Maybe that divorce took everything from you, or that storm took away everything you worked hard for. Life has a way of humbling us and pushing us to our knees before God.

Even though life turned against these men, they did not elect to be a victim. They did not make their new condition of being homeless a contented place but rather they used it as a platform to push themselves out, even if it meant taking some risks. They were not afraid of trying. How many times in our lives have we been fearful of trying again because we have failed once or a few times? Maybe one marriage failed, and we make that our benchmark and vow that we will never marry or even cuss the whole species because one did us harm. These men did not think of themselves as a failure in their mind, even though everything around them were negative. They thought positive in their mind, saw an image or a vision of where they wanted to be and spoke it out declaring it in agreement.

Decisions will either hold us back or free us to fly

They said, "If we say we'll go into the city, the famine is there, and we will die. And if we stay here, we will die. So, let's go over to the camp of the Arameans and surrender. If they spare us, we live; if they kill us, then we die," 2 Kings 7:4 NIV.

They did not have a lot of options, so they debated and took a chance as they had nothing to lose.

1. If they stayed where they were, they would die without food and water,

2. If they went back into the city, they would be killed.

3. If they went to the next city, they would be killed also but *perhaps* they would find mercy.

Sometimes in life, we have to decide where we want to be and what we want to do otherwise we will never leave where we are.

The Bible says, that these four men **decided** that they did not want to be where they were and made up their mind to get out and be somewhere else. Taking a chance can be a startling experience especially if we have had recurrent failures. No one is totally certain about any decision. Every decision has some form of risk involved. Sometimes when we are absolutely fed up in a situation, it can assist in the initiation of a decision. Fear will hold us back, but like these men, we must take that step forward, feeling the fear but not allowing it to control us. We will never find out what our future holds if we allow our current situation to defeat us. Just as a tiny spark of fire can burn the whole city down, in the same way, all we need is a little bit of hope and faith and let God do the rest. You may be in a season of hope but unable to recognize it because it looks like a problem. Nothing is what it looks like from outside, everything is an illusion. Everything we go through in life leaves us with an experience, lessons we may not have learnt any other way.

I would not have come to Australia, met all the lovely people, made a career for myself and toured the world, if I had given up hope completely thinking that God was punishing me by putting me in that dreadful situation. I had to take a chance because I too lost everything that mattered to me, but it was not the end, it was just the beginning of something new. Circumstances threw the lady with the Alabaster Jar in a job that was not sustaining her. She had an invisible hope that spoke deep within her telling her that her circumstance was a lie, it was not permanent. She knew somehow that Jesus was bigger than her problem, that there was something in Him that she needed. Her context gave her material benefits, but deep down she was still searching for wholeness, for something that completed her, and she found that in Jesus. Sometimes we must speak to that circumstance in our lives, telling it that it was a lie, that it was not going to stay, that there was an upgrade coming, that the GPS of our lives was rerouting in any moment, taking us to our destiny.

There is more for you

When you take the next step, something will break in your favor.

Life can throw us sicknesses, challenges, and troubles in our path, but the decision of how we react to these is left solely on us. We are the ones sitting on the driver's seat. We cannot blame others for the choices and the mistakes we have made. Yes, perhaps others had a part to play in our lives, and our bad situations, but the decision to rise above those situations has been handed to us alone.

We can decide if we want to stay a victim or become a survivor. It is essential to learn from our bad situations and mistakes, forgiving ourselves and agreeing to move forward, making something of ourselves. God has given us all a gift of choice. We choose every day and our choices make us or break us. Today is a gift given to us, and by God's wisdom and help, we can make the right choices today, as the Bible says in Proverbs 20:24, that a good man's steps are directed by the Lord and in Proverbs 16:9, it says that although we may make plans, God determines our steps, He sets our pace.

I am hoping that each strategy we make is God's plan for our lives and every step is a step of faith and in His wisdom, only then we can be fruitful in all we do.

Although for many years I made brokenness my excuse and accepted my fate, a day came when something inside confronted me and I had to decide to stay and die or to get out and live. It wasn't easy for God to give up His own son as well, and it wasn't easy for Jesus to take the sins of every human being on his body. The devil likes nothing more than keeping us in bondage, helplessness and in lack all our lives where all our dreams die; and we become his slave. Today I am grateful how far God has brought me from the days I was begging for bread. I put myself through university while working as a caregiver at night, pushed to make something of myself and become independent, fought depression and anxiety, missed my son who had died and my other boy who I lost in divorce, cried a lot, made some poor decisions but slowly by God's grace I am here today sharing with you the mosaic of my life. God was enough in me. Maybe in the shadows of the struggles of my past, you may be able to find strength and courage to do something you wanted to do even when everything might look dead in your life. There is always hope, love and redemption in Christ Jesus, freely given to us and freely we must give also.

It is not what it looks like

It was winter in Melbourne and I was taking a walk to clear my head. My heart was heavy as I had numerous issues that I was concerned about. I walked past a dead looking tree. Its branches were barren. I walked past that tree numerous times, few times in a week in fact. This time as I walked past, I heard a whisper, 'Come and look closer.' As I walked on, ignoring what I thought I heard, I distinctively heard it speak to me again. I stopped startled at first, and there it was again, a silent voice summoning me to come closer and have a look. I stood still for a moment and then I was curious, so I retraced my steps and treading closer to the tree, I looked meticulously. I heard a murmur in my spirit that winter was over. I had to categorically look persistently because at first, I was not certain what I was beholding, and then I saw miniscule buds appearing. I heard in my spirit, that although the tree may look barren now but look closer, winter was over. You may have been in barrenness for a season but come forward and look closer, your winter is over. I heard God say in my spirit to speak to the dead things in my life, to those dead dreams and hopes and tell it that winter was over, to wake up. Things that you gave up on because of lack of resources, lack of money, or because they said you could not do it, that you were not smart enough, God is saying, speak to that dead drying thing in your life and tell it that your winter was over. See life coming in all those dead areas in your life because Jesus is the resurrection and the life.

Despite our mistakes, God can still use us and make things right, for there is nothing too hard for God. God told Lot's wife when leaving Sodom and Gomorrah, not to look back at the fire coming down from Heaven to destroy the cities. Look back only to see how far God has brought you. If we look back long enough, the murmurs of the past will flirt with us, drawing us closer with its sweet lies, beckoning us to return. Look ahead, everything God has for you is ahead of you, not behind. Keep your focus on the promise of God for your life, even though it may appear to be delayed, but don't worry or fret, stay in faith because it will surely come to pass at the chosen time that God has allocated.

We all make plans for our life; a great job, the picket fence and rose garden, the perfect spouse and well-behaved children, but what if none of it comes true? When we merge our plans with God's plan for our lives, we find a deeper fulfillment in all we do. We can go through life discontent in all we do, searching for an outside purpose without realizing that it is inside of us. Once we realize this truth and seek out to find our purpose, we will never be the same again, because every pain we went through in life starts to make sense. It is a good feeling when you finally find your purpose and walk in it.

God says in Jeremiah 29:11 NIV, "For I know the plans I have for you, the plans to prosper you and not to harm you, the plans to give you the future you are hoping for."

I tried to do life in my own terms, without God, but it did not take very long for me to decide that I could not do anything without God. He designed us in such a way that we are part of Him, and without Him, we are not complete. I needed Him like I required air to breathe. How could I live without breathing? Our breath is His breath. "Then Lord God formed a man from the dust of the ground and breathed into his nostrils the breath of life, and the man became a living being," Genesis 2:7 NIV. I needed God to be able to breathe. Denying Him was choosing death.

Chapter Four
Envy is a Deception

We tend to hate our body and start to envy other people when we have gone through personal trauma. We look longingly at people who appear better than us, perhaps wear nicer clothes, and live in nice houses. We want to be everyone else but us.

Trauma and loss of any kind can leave us with deep scars. It could be a scar of shame, lack of self-worth and anger. It habitually affects emotional, mental and physical well-being. Many women and men who have suffered any form of personal trauma like sexual abuse, domestic violence or mental breakdown, find it difficult to share their stories. It takes a lot of courage to expose your scar to strangers. That is why it is imperative to be empathetic, thoughtful and nonjudgmental in their healing process and recognize that everyone heals differently in their own space. Women most times may be able to share their pain with another person or in a contained safe group environment, but for men, it is difficult to open to anyone about their pain. They may suffer in silence which often leads to depression and even suicide.

When we have been violated, we often go through a profound shame. We may question and even blame ourselves. Total shame and self-loath is probably the lowest vibration we would feel after a traumatic experience. I hated my body, the way I looked and felt. I was very critical. I looked in the mirror and detested what I saw. I wanted to die. I washed several times to sanitize myself. I felt dirty all the time. I was afraid of men. I jumped when anyone was brash or spoke loud around me. I became fearful of a lot of things, a door shutting loudly, phone ringing, knock on the door, I suffered anxiety from abuse. Everyone around me was oblivious to my impediments. I could not sleep at night for a long time. This is when people develop an eating disorder. I was emaciated and hated my body. Some people cut themselves to express their inner pain. Abused people attract abusive relationships because they feel a sense of connection to brokenness, a feeling of home. Broken people think that no one else will have them, that they are not enough for a wholesome healthy relationship and not worthy of any good thing. They feel dejected, cast-off, lonely and unloved. This is where people feel lost and hopeless and abuse illicit substances to manage the inner pain and to escape the war that might be going on the inside of their mind. Anger is a way to cope, a progression from shame in the healing process. Anger can become very disruptive if not directed sensibly. I was angry with myself for not protecting myself. I had this inner rage which had the potential to become dangerous if not guided carefully. At times I wanted to destroy everything and everyone around me. I wanted the world to pay for what happened to me. I was angry with myself and with men. I blamed every other man for what one man did to me. Anger can make you blame everyone around you, even the innocent who did not hurt you. You judge everyone, spitting your anger toward everyone. You initially don't care who you hurt, you lash out on people who display kindness and love. An abused person can be rude and hurtful for no reason. We put a mask showing that we are okay but when no one is looking we are vulnerable and teary. We are screaming on the inside, but no one hears us. We cannot find ways to share our inner turmoil, our pain and to heal. We tell ourselves that it is not a big deal, that other people have gone through worse things than us, to get over it but we don't know how to. There is no psychology or counseling that goes deep enough to touch those raw bleeding areas inside us but God.

What's meant to be yours is yours

We start envying other people who seem wholesome and wish we were like them, unblemished and untarnished. We don't want to be us anymore because it hurts too much to be us. We want what looks good on others, but it is not what God wants us to have, so we imitate, we pretend, and we lie to ourselves. God will give you what is yours, you do not have to be like anyone else. Your experiences can speak life in someone else's life who might feel like they are drowning.

Envy is a deception sent from the pits of hell to keep us in longing and in want, and not appreciating the moment God has given us and already done for us.

With envy comes jealousy and with jealousy comes temptation, ungratefulness and sin. When we long for things that we don't have and become preoccupied with longing, it keeps our focus from pursuing our own goals and dreams and that was what the enemy wanted for me, to keep me away from my God-given purpose, and from identifying what God had for me. When we long for things others have, envying other people's possessions, lifestyle or talents, it can trap us into a prison of being in want and ungratefulness.

We look for ways to get those things in the wrong quick way, and not God's way.

The enemy comes subtly, little thought at a time, presenting nice things, trying to justify why we should have them, telling us that God did not care about us, otherwise He would have given them to us. He brings situations in our lives that cause us to doubt Gods love and provision.

The devil will tell us his easy ways to make money to obtain what we desire and once we start to imagine doing it his way, our actions follow, and it becomes reality. It will rob us of peace and joy when we go after that which is not ours.

The Bible says the enemy comes for one purpose only, that is to steal, kill and destroy (see John 10:10).

He does not love us, feel sorry for us, or care about us.

When we don't like ourselves, and how God sees us and what His word says about us, we imitate other people we admire and dress like them but inside we are hurting and confused. We wonder why we seem to be the only one suffering while others around us seem to be having a good time, enjoying their lives. Internal hurts can bring confusion in many areas and one of them is identity. If we have lost a father early in our lives, we grow up confused because we don't see a role model in our lives; we don't have a father to go to. We search in the wrong places for that love only a father or mother could give. We end up in places doing things we should not do and trusting people who lead us astray. We start to see ourselves through the eyes of people who are as confused and broken as we are, and we allow them in our lives; we put our trust in them to lead us which may even provide a way to escape from our own pain and reality initially, but then we get deeper in sin and we have no control of our lives and decisions and are unable to get out of bondage. It may seem harmless and fun at first, but it leads us into deeper sin in doing things we are forced to do, from where we cannot escape without supernatural help.

We want things and we push boundaries to attain them.

The Bible says the devil is a liar (see John 8:44), he will tell us to go after things we desire that is not ours, in whichever way we can, even at times to stop giving tithe and offering and use that money to buy substances we desire, after all, everyone is doing it, that God does not mind us having nice things. And when we do stop to listen to the lies of the devil and take easy ways out, he will come back to convict and put guilt on us. He is a master at deceiving and many times we fall in his trap and get misled but if we have Gods Word embedded in us, we will be able to identify that it is not God for it is written; "My sheep hear my voice, and I know them, and they follow me," John 10:27-28 KJV.

I am glad God is a merciful God who forgives us even when we have been undeserving and unfaithful to Him.

When we complain about what other people have and what we don't have and compare other people's wealth or their talents and looks, we are saying to God that we are not happy with what he has given us and that he is not a good provider. The Bible says that when we seek things of the Lord, He will make all grace abound toward us. He will direct us to gain wealth and will cause us to be at the right place at the right time, to meet the right people who will bless us. We can use the anger of our past hurts and channel it to elevate ourselves for greater purpose where we can help others to overcome their fears and hurts. I would ask God why He allowed me to be hurt. I was naïve and didn't know the truth about myself, that I was made in God's image and that I was enough no matter what had happened to me or who had hurt me. He knew us before we were conceived in our mother's womb and called us the apple of His eye. He loves you and me and we are enough without anything else, without qualifications, or experiences, job or no job, degree or no degree, we are enough just being us with all our loses, hopes and dreams and all our baggage. The Bible says in John 8: 32 NIV, "You shall know the truth, and the truth shall set you free." The truth is that we are wonderfully and fearfully made in the image of God (see Psalm 139), and everything that happens in the middle does not really matter because God has our past, our present and our future in the palm of His hands.

Power of visualization

We can imagine the good things God has for us in His word and use that to pull ourselves out of the difficult hurtful places.

To get my healing from my past hurts, I meditated on the scriptures of the Bible like an ointment to my broken areas. I spoke to my circumstances, diseases and dark places while using positive visualization. When I took a step out in faith to start the ministry God spoke to me about, I would get dressed in my best work clothes in the morning, put my make up on and my heels as if I was going to work, except I had no job. I bought a small computer desk and chair from a garage sale even though I had no computer and created a space in the corner between our very small dining room and kitchen and believed that was my office. I even took a lunch break. Our God listens to the crazy type of radical prayers and faith that says, God, I can feel it, smell it and see it manifest in my life. God is moved by radical faith. Imagination produces results, good or bad; it produces after its own kind.

My story may sound a bit extreme, but our God is extreme. He told a wrinkled old impotent man who was fatherless to believe for a child. God's promise made Abraham hopeful in his hopeless situation, creating an image in his mind of being a father. Do you think they ever doubted when nothing changed in their life to show that God's promise was real? Waiting for the manifestation of Gods promise is not easy. Many of us have given up and taken the easy way out. I am sure the devil sniggered at them and told them all sorts of lies, that they were crazy for trusting God in something that was hopeless and dead. But they took God at His word and did all that God asked them to do.

God used imagination as a tool that helped Abraham to keep his faith in God on the promise that was given to him. He took him outside and said, "Look up at the sky and count the stars, if indeed you can count them," Genesis 15: 5 NIV. Then he said to him, "So shall your offspring be." I am certain that every time Abraham found himself depressed and discouraged because what God promised him did not transpire immediately, he looked up at the stars and visualized having as many children and believed. He declared God's promise over Himself repeatedly till it become real in his spirit when he 'saw' what God displayed to him. That is how powerful imagination is; when you visualize where you want to be, plan and take steps, you will get there. It grew so big on the inside of him that it finally became real in his life.

Whatever you *imagine* and *see* in your mind's eye, you will eventually become. Good or bad, your imagination will become real. Faith and Fear work in the same way. They both imagine and believe that which is not there yet. Even though you have had a bad experience, it is not your destiny and it does not outline who you are. Bad things happened to good people in the Bible. Job lost all his children, his extensive agricultural empire, his vast investments and assets, and his livelihood, even then he kept his faith up. Naomi also in the book of Ruth lost her two children and her husband, but Gods thoughts and ways are higher than ours and He is well able to rebuild us to better than what we had before.

Some strongholds do not break easily. In fact, in the Bible in the Gospel of Mark and Matthew, it is recorded that the disciples could not cast out a particular demon when previously they were successful in casting out demons and strongholds. When they asked Jesus the reason why they could not do it this time, Jesus explained that it was essential to use prayer and faith together with some kinds of demons and generational strongholds. Somethings in our life have been there for a long time, even generations, and it will not leave easily.

The Bible expresses to us to fetch those imaginations and everything else that holds us a prisoner and remove it, cast it out, replace it with positive declarations and visualisations, (see 2 Corinthians 10:15).

We must consciously capture each thought as it comes and pull it down and answer it with the Word of God. When we learn to recognize thoughts that are not of God it becomes easier to replace them with positive ones. Learn to question yourself, "Why am I thinking this way, is it from God, why am I confused, God doesn't send confusion?"

Every day we are surrounded by things, electricity, buildings, cars, technology, computers, airplanes but we forget that all those things started from a thought. Every man-made object you see was created from a thought, an idea. I used to lie awake thinking and imagining my ministry, saw myself preaching in front of thousands of people, many walking away restored before I was even invited to speak anywhere. Our thoughts become imaginations that develop into goals and plans and finally translate into drawings, business plans, building designs on the paper which eventually manifest into real things. The Bible says, "For as he thinks in his heart, so is he," (Proverbs 23:7 NKJV).

When we think weak thoughts of hopelessness, sickness and pain, thoughts of self-pity that make us sad; those thoughts become images in our mind and manifests in our lives. When we regularly tear ourselves down; we will become powerless and feel hopeless and will be too afraid to try anything new. The Bible says the prodigal son talked himself into returning home after making a bad choice (see Luke 15:11-32). First, he thought in his mind, then he spoke it out loud, then it manifested into actions that brought reconciliation in his life.

How often we try to negotiate with ourselves into not undertaking things that God has called us to do because of false claims of our inability. If you think big powerful thoughts that make you feel big on the inside, then you can talk yourself into achieving the impossible.

Our positive thoughts and imaginations can empower us to overcome obstacles in our life the same way it can pull us down into a dark hole of depression.

When we get symptoms of pain or discomfort in our body, the devil will whisper thoughts into our head that we have an illness, perhaps even a deadly disease and if we entertain these thoughts long enough, we will start to imagine ourselves becoming worse. The more we think about it, we begin to feel the pain as our imagination causes those thoughts to manifest and when we go to the doctor our worst fear is confirmed. But if we train ourselves to capture the negative thoughts initially and pull them off from its roots and speaking God's word over that pain or sickness, it would bow its knee and die. It has no other way but to do what it has been told to do in Jesus mighty powerful Name.

I have had many instances where the devil had lied about pain on my body, and I had to stop and declare God's Word repeatedly, till that pain and symptom left my body. It did not leave straight away, sometimes I had to stand on the Word of God for months before healing manifested. The enemy tries our faith by pushing us to the maximum, just to see how long we will stand. Healing is already ours, but we must stand on our faith till it becomes apparent in our lives, as the devil will not just hand it to us. God's Word will never let us down if we believe and are prepared to stand.

I had a breast cancer scare in 2016 just when I had moved interstate chasing after my purpose. I had a recall from a breast mammogram as an area of abnormality was identified. I did not suffer any discomfort, had no lumps or pain. It came as a total surprise and immediately fear entered my mind and it formed an image of death. Most times the first emotion we feel is dread at the face of adversity or bad news.

From the moment of the recall letter in the mail till post-surgery, night and day I struggled to fight the fear and the thoughts of death and dying. Some nights I could not sleep, and other nights I woke up in cold sweats, pacing the floor of my lounge in the winter months declaring healing scriptures from the Bible. I was afraid of the upcoming surgery. I paced the floor crying and praying to God asking if there was any other way. I found myself repeating it in tears. Then I saw Jesus alone in the garden of Mt Gethsemane, crying the same prayer to God, (Matthew 26), I heard God speak in my spirit, "Jesus is the way, the bridge to the other side." The spiritual warfare was waging in my mind and visualizing anything good was difficult at that time, as all I could see was what the devil was showing me. It was the fear and the thoughts that I was fighting. I wrestled to pull down images of death and dying that the devil was showing me. I did not want to die without completing Gods purpose for my life. I had just found my calling and had given up everything to pursue it. I was not about to let the devil take it away from me. I told myself that God would not have given me the ministry if He had planned for me to die. I imagined myself preaching in huge auditoriums. I screenshot some preaching of other preachers and used a photo writing app to write my name over it. I looked at it over and over till I could see myself on that platform instead of them. I refused to accept what the devil had thrown on me, then one day the Holy Spirit gently rose up inside of me bringing me to realize that it was only the enemy trying to scare me. I stood on the Word of God for each thought and fought hard in the spirit, pulling one thought at a time and replacing each thought with what the Word of God said about me and what His promises were over my life. I read His prophetic word over and over. I wrote down healing scriptures on my phone and meditated on them. I was determined to do whatever it took to get my health back. I told my self that Jesus had won the battle and He had given me healing. I still had to have the surgery and God was there with me. I was no longer afraid. God's peace had come, and I knew deep down I was okay.

Chapter Five
The Mind is the Powerhouse.

Our mind does not need a passport to travel? It can go anywhere anytime and leave us behind. We can be sitting in the most beautiful place, surrounded by our loved ones and still not enjoy the moment because of that one niggling thought about a past matter which could discreetly pay a visit and sabotage the present moment.

The devil targets those who are a threat to him, he doesn't mind us going to church as long as we don't build a close relationship with Jesus. He is okay with us falling asleep in church or day dreaming.

He comes to feed into our mind with the movie of our past, of what someone alleged long time ago, opinions of others, offenses and rebelliousness and retain us in his territory, occupied in worry and fear till we forget we ever had a purpose in life. He is very crafty but if we learn how he works we will be better equipped to recognize his tactics.

Thoughts and afflictions will come, people will talk about us and tell dreadful lies, but it is often how we react to those words that matter. We can accept it or reject it by replying with God's word. When we reject those thoughts that creep into our mind and do not accept it, the devil will not be able to pull us down. It is only when we receive it then it becomes a problem because we allow it to marinate in our mind and like a curd that the cow chews, we bring it back and forth till we become very upset and sick. We spend more time worrying about it than spending time in the word or in prayer and worship.

The Bible in Genesis describes how talking to yourself and acting on your thoughts makes things happen. God talked to Himself (the father, son and the holy spirit), when He made man in his own image. "Then God said,

"Let us make mankind in our image, in our likeness," Genesis 1:26 NIV. God designed us like Himself, where we have to talk things into being.

In order to make things happen, we need to;

Think it, speak it, act it!

Instead of allowing our mind which is the powerhouse of our body to have its own way of bringing things up from the past, we can control it by turning on our worship. Things don't have to be perfect in our life for us to start worshipping and thanking God. If we don't have a car and must catch a bus, thank Him that we can get out of our house and are able to catch the bus, as there are many who are not able to leave their house. We always have a reason to praise. We always have something to be grateful for. And when we stop murmuring and start worshipping, God presents Himself into the little we have and makes it plentiful. Don't be like the children of Israel, who murmured and complained themselves out of their promise, and angered God, (see Exodus 16: 2; Numbers 14:27).

Our thought matters

The enemy attacks our mind, that's where we win or lose any battle before we even begin to fight. When we give up in our mind, we lose the battle. I nearly gave up on this book many times as it all seemed too hard. I used to talk myself out of job interviews because the more I imagined three-panel interview, six eyes glaring at me and judging me, the more self-conscious I became, and I would not turn up for the interview.

Fear stopped me from trying. If I presented to the interview, I would have at least had a chance to get the job. But because fear stopped me from going, I allowed the enemy to rob me from what could have been mine, from finances and from self-confidence.

Our mind is the greatest resource, and the enemy knows that if he messes up with our mind by negative thoughts, fear and worry, he can take control of our destiny.

The thoughts that consumed my mind were negative, of being dirty, of not being worthy, that I should not live. Just as people judged the lady with the Alabaster Jar and called her names without getting to know the real her, I was also constantly worried that if people found out that I had a secret of being molested, they would not be my friend or would look at me as if I had leprosy. As I grew older and lived in domestic violence, I did not want people to know that my husband was beating me up. I covered it up with lies. Like many other people in domestic violence, I would lie that I knocked myself against a wall or had a fall that was why I had a bruise. Broken people often don't have friends as they prefer to be alone so that they don't have to explain anything to anybody. Often my past would creep in my mind and would try to destroy my present. Sometimes we feel emotions of longing, loss, abandonment, rejection, and don't know where it is coming from or why we feel the way we do. We may feel like crying but don't know why; we have this heaviness we cannot explain.

I left Fiji and did not return to my country for more than twenty years because I was afraid of my past. It reminded me of my heart-wrenching cries, the face of my dying child, my bed that was tainted by other women, the pain and losses from my decision to choose man before God. God took me back after many years to face my giants before His plan could manifest in my life. I needed to forgive. Only when I let go, I was able to heal.

Whatever you are going through in your life and in your family, as much as it hurts, and as lonely as you feel, remember it is not about you. It is a spiritual warfare where your mind and your thought life are under an attack from satan who is more afraid of you than you are of him. It is a mind game he plays with us, testing our faith.

I spent more time thinking negative poor me, why me kind of thoughts, worrying about many things that I had no control of, visualizing the worse than positive can-do thoughts and this category of thoughts and imaginations held me in reserve with fear and lack for many years and robbed me of joy, of love and of every good things that God had for me. Paul teaches us (see *Ephesians 6:10-18)*, how to fight spiritual warfare.

Today we have at hand a variety of online resources, books, and phone applications that teach faith.

As a child, I loved reading the Bible and imagined being in all the places I was reading about. It also improved my English and God used my childlike faith to bring salvation and healing to people even when I was young.

We try to fill the void in us for acceptance by continuing a silent pursuit for inner peace searching in material things, projects, sex, drug, alcohol but we fail to find it except when we come to Jesus who gives a kind of peace the world cannot give us. Sometimes we think a man or a woman, a partner can fill the void in us, but we soon find out that nothing can fill that longing, the emptiness in our heart, except God himself because in Him we are complete, we are whole, we are one. God does not give love. He is love. When we get Him, we get love, peace, joy, wellness, wealth, healing and redemption, the whole lot, because He cannot separate Himself.

We may work hard at a project but if it is not from God, we may not find peace in it even if it was successful.

Have you ever emptied yourself to a special mission that had been close to your heart or given your all to perhaps an exam, a job promotion, or a business but did not accomplish what you expected? Maybe a promotion that was promised to you and you worked very hard for it and it went to someone else less deserving and you felt unhappy, discouraged and upset. I had a young family and a full-time job while I studied full time as well. I had put much effort into my education to attain a degree in nursing, but when it was all over, I did not feel any excitement, because the cost of my accomplishment was higher than I had anticipated; juggling studies, young family and a full-time job. There is always a cost attached to something of value.

With all my achievements I still felt empty. I wore a suit and high heel shoes and looked confident on the outside but behind all that cover was a little girl frightened of the dark, intimidated by other women, anxious around men, afraid to fall sleep.

I worked especially hard to make up for those lost years that I was in domestic violence. I was in a hurry to make something of myself.

I picked up double shifts to chase after material things, objects that take our focus away from God and eventually become our God. God says, have no other Gods before me (see Deuteronomy 5:7). When we put our hope in the worldly things, we never find the fulfilment we are craving for, because we keep wanting more.

Make a decision to worship God regardless

One decision changed the course of my life, the decision to reconcile with my childhood God.

When all that I had set out to achieve fell apart in my life, my rebelliousness was on my face. Job said in Job 42:5 NIV, "My ears had heard of you but now my eyes have seen you." I went through terrible trials and only then I was able to see the hand of God move powerfully in my life. I understood what it was like to submit to God completely and trust Him for my every need. I learned to praise Him when I had nothing, just a bag of hand me down clothes. Prophet Habakkuk in Habakkuk 3:17 NIV state, "Though the fig tree does not bud and there are no grapes on the vines, even though the olive crops fail, and the field shall not yield any meat, the flock shall be cut off from the fold, and there shall be no herd in the stall yet will I praise Him."

I praise Him not because I have, but because who He is. He is powerful and mighty, and He showed me that no matter how small and insignificant I felt, how lost and alone I was, when I opened my mouth to worship Him, He came like a sun shining in the darkness of my life. To God, I give all Glory for where He has brought me today.

When we are tested of time, when we think we have failed God and ourselves and messed things up gravely, dejected we may want to go back to what had been familiar to us, that which sustained us even if it was a place of brokenness. Peter in the Bible was an entrepreneur who displayed exceptional skills in his fishing career when Jesus found him. He had commendable abilities of a hardworking man with strong hands and a well-toned body being out in the sun and the wind. He was brave as well going out sailing in the rough seas with fishermen who were equally strong and rough like him. He was the one who had put his hand out to strike and cut the ear of a soldier when they came to arrest Jesus. Jesus loved Peter despite all his faults, (see Luke 22: 54-62). When Peter realized what he had done denying Jesus, he was crushed by his own action, felt broken and deeply remorseful. Crying bitterly, he walked away from his ministry doubting about his ability to continue. Sometimes when we have made a mistake that has cost us more than we estimated, we tend to doubt if we were ever called to venture in that project or our calling. When my son was dying in front of me, I was nineteen years old, sitting alone at his crib, hoping I died with him. I felt extremely overwhelmed, very alone and hopeless. I had nothing inside of me to draw strength from, but what the enemy meant bad for me, God turned it around for something good. Sometimes when we have stepped out in faith to whatever God has called us to do, leaving our past behind, and if it does not work out the way we expected, it is easier to give up and return to our old ways because it is familiar.

Our subconscious mind holds pictures of our past and always draws us back even for a moment. Certain smell or a place may take us right back to something that happened in the past. I was a victim of abuse for many years and the reason abused people stay in bad relationships even when they know it is hurting them and the children, is because they are not able to change their mindset. Their subconscious minds pull them back to the belief that they are loved in a strange way, because after the abuse, the abuser often makes up with flowers and kind acts, telling them how much they are loved, and that they both cannot live without each other. Even when the victim leaves, they often return because in some strange way they believe they are loved and cannot live without their abuser. The abuser always blames the victim for making them angry, that it was all their fault that they got the beating. The abused person tries very hard to please them in every way but always falls short. Over time they become dependent on their abuser because it has been repeatedly expressed to them that they would be alone and helpless without their abuser, that no one else would love them the way they are being loved and if only they didn't make the abuser angry, behaved in a certain way, dressed in a certain way, all would be well. The victim believes the lies and because their self-esteem is already low, they stay in the relationship. They have nowhere else to go, they have no resources or money, and they lack confidence in themselves to start something new or to get a job. The abuser slowly isolates them from all their friends and families till the victim is totally reliant on the abuser for everything. The abuser controls what they wear, where they go, who they see, they will not even leave them alone with the doctor. The victim starts to believe that the abuse is what they deserve because they have been bad. They don't realize that it is a lie from the pits of hell. You can't profess to love someone and beat them mercilessly, but for some strange reason, the abuser thinks they love the person they are trying to hurt and control. They may even feel remorseful afterwards, and often promise it will not occur again, and perhaps even mean it, but it continues and despite what the abuser does to them, the victim feels obligated to stay. I too stayed for all those reasons.

I was feeling all that Peter was feeling, disappointed, tested of time, wanting to give up, hated myself for not trusting God, denying Jesus in my life and going my own way. I was angry that I had given up so much and received nothing in return. God found me when I was planning suicide. Isn't it amusing how God comes not a fraction late, just on time before your head sinks in the water and you drown, almost like when you are standing on the cliff and about to fall, He shows up not a minute early and not a minute late? He saw my tears and my loneliness, and His small voice whispered deep inside of me like an impression, promising never to leave me nor abandon me, (see Deuteronomy31:6).

Even though I had lost everything in the storms of my life, God had not shifted, He was still faithful to His word, reminding me that He still had me in the palm of His mighty hands, and He has you and we can create again with our creator father.

When I started to become what He had called me to be, I stopped being a people pleaser and ceased to care about what others thought of me. I felt complete in my intimacy with God. He wants us to forsake all the things that hold us back, the voices from our past, and chase after Him, like we do when we are young and foolish and blindly in love.

Life will teach us lessons that no education, no degree, and no teacher can teach. Life has many ups and downs, valleys and mountains, like walking barefooted on a gravel road in the heat and rain. Storms will come and threaten to take away all that we have built, and there will be times when we are walking alone and other times walking with people, but when we are firmly anchored in Christ Jesus, He will hold our hand and walk with us because He has gone on this journey before us.

The devil knows our vulnerabilities and launches his attack right on the spot where we are weak.

Have you ever been secretly depressed, miserable and unhappy? You go to work, you smile appropriately and engage in conversations politely, but no one suspects your inner turmoil. I was secretly miserable, even with of all my achievements, I felt I was not complete, that nothing I did was good enough, I always fell short. I was looking for my purpose but in the wrong places. I always talked myself down. The biggest goal I had was to get married before I was twenty years old, because in my culture then if a girl was not married by twenty years of age, people gossiped and made up rumors that there could be something wrong with that girl that was why no one was marrying them. It sounds silly now, but I come for a culture where a girl's sole purpose was to get married and please her husband and his families. I am glad it is changing now where girls are encouraged to become whatever they desire.

God gave me a second chance in life, he gave me a God loving husband who loves and cares for me and my children and allowed me to become whatever God had for me. I became successful but kept chasing for more to find validation and endorsement because it was difficult for me initially to change my mindset. It took me a long time to accept my new life and feel the freedom to run after what God had for me. We can have everything new and still live in our past by allowing the whispers of our past to suppress us. We bring all our excess baggage into a new relationship and may not even know it. We become highly suspicious because of what happened to us in the previous relationship. We don't give our new relationship a fresh start. Because we have not changed our mindset. We have walked in a new thing with an old mindset. Unless we learn to modify our thought pattern, deal with our past issues and cut it off completely, burn the bridge that leads to our past, we will not be able to fully embrace the new.

Sometimes people may place us through an interrogation about our past and question God's calling in our lives, but God does not see any of these things that people see. When God dispenses to us an assignment, He does not base it on our past or our strength and failures. In fact, in the Bible God always seemed to use people who did not have enough, the discarded people, the ones who had sinful past and had no appropriate skills or qualifications. When God called me, I told Him that He had made a mistake, that I was empty and did not have anything to bring to Him. I did not come from a lineage of preachers in my family nor had I any money. For everything in my life, I had to rely on God completely. I had no eloquence of words and no theology degree. The only theology certificates I had, were from my childhood days of correspondence Bible College. I did not know anything about calling or gifts. All I knew was I had a strong pull toward God, an insatiable hunger that made me seek Him out. He had apprehended me like He did Paul in the Bible. I could not hide from Him, wherever I went He was on my face till I accepted my calling.

It took many years of pain, tears, and brokenness for the fragrance that He had placed inside of me to come out.

You have a purpose, a calling, a testimony that can only come out with a fragrance after it has been broken at the master's feet. I am grateful to God for all He is doing in my life because when we have a grateful heart, it pleases God and He downloads His blessing onto us.

When the children of Israel mumbled and complained in Numbers 14:28, God told them that they will get the very thing God heard them say. They did not enter the promised land. Be careful what comes out of your mouth, because what you say has power. When we fill our mind with positive declarations, listen to preaching that empowers us, we will be able to overcome the plots and plans of the enemy.

Chapter Six
When God is Quiet

What to do when God is quiet, and we are in SOS, we need Him urgently and God is not saying anything? Why does He not answer, or are we asking the wrong question?

You are in a crisis, your rent is due, your child is sick, you are about to lose your job, your marriage is over, you have lost your business, you cried to God, fasted and prayed, and God did not show up at the meeting. You feel alone, hurt and ashamed. You counted on God to turn up, but He did not show up. You did the faith thing, invited Him to the meeting, waited and looked at your watch and you looked at the door but no sign of God. You placed all your bet on Him, and He did not come to the party, or so it seemed. You are disappointed, and angry for believing and trusting a God you had not seen, you feel let down, that one time you needed God; He too let you down just like everyone else had done. Based on that assumption you decide to leave this 'Christian thing' and go back to your past. We compare God to everyone else in our lives that let us down, but God is not like everyone else. God is awesome and sees the end from the beginning and if our prayer did not get answered the way we expected it to, it is because God loves us and wants the best for us. Some doors He must close for our benefit because our vision is too small. If He had not closed some doors in my life, I would not be here writing this book and ministering to people.

God will not stop your opponents, but He will equip you

Just because things did not work out the way we expected, instead of going back to that which has been holding us in the past, to those friends and habits and to the old ways, we must continue to push toward our goal. What God has done in my life is far more than what I lost.

God answers all our prayers, He sees tears before a drop falls onto our cheek, but never the way we expect Him to. He is always in our storm, after all, He was the fourth man in the fiery furnace (see Daniel 3:25), He looked like a ghost walking on the water (see Matthew 14:26); He was mistaken as a gardener (see John 20:15); He was sleeping in the boat during the storm (see Mark 4:38), He is the lily of the valley and He is the Great I AM.

He is a present help in time of trouble (see Psalm 46:1).

He has said in His Word that He hears us when we call Him, "Call upon me in the day of trouble and I will deliver you," (Psalm 50:15 NIV)

We expect him to come to our situation and hold the door open, the door that He may be trying to close because maybe we have outgrown our time there. He comes to the meeting but instead of keeping the door open, He shuts it because our season in that job is over. He is leading us to the next phase of our life, pushing us out to our next season of blessing.

He did not stop Joseph from being sold by his brothers, but He went ahead of him and prepared a way and used him to bless the whole family and the nation later when the country went through a serious famine (see Genesis 37:12-36). God goes ahead of us to prepare what we don't see.

You might be going through a situation right now as you are reading this but rest assured that God has gone ahead of you to fight the battle for you. When King Jehoshaphat in 2 Chronicles 20, was afraid of the large robust army that was approaching to fight his Empire, he called a national prayer and consulted God. God heard their cry and told them not to be afraid but to go ahead into the battle and God would give them victory. God did not stop the battle, nor did He tell them not to go. They had to step out in faith into the battle. Sometimes God will lead us into battle and require us to trust in His strength. King Jehoshaphat did something very strange to honor God, he placed in front of his army a prayer and worship team and commanded everyone to march forward singing praises to God. As they advanced toward the battleground, God had sent an ambush ahead of them and avenged their enemies for them. You can go ahead into any situation you are facing today with a firm confirmation that God has gone ahead of you to fight for you.

God turned Joseph's bad situation around and used the very thing that looked like a problem, to bless a humble little family and made them into a great wealthy nation, called Israel. The very thing the enemy sent to hurt you, God will turn it around to bless you and bring Him Glory.

I went through a series of hardship and trials in my life and during those seasons, I begged God to take me out, to avenge my enemies and although it seemed like didn't come to get me out, when I looked back and on hindsight, I could see how it all worked out for His glory and for my good. I am glad He did not take me out of those situations because of in those dark moments, like a seed, my faith grew and produced fruits. When I came out on the other side, I was no longer that same person, because the dark moments had not only transformed me, but it has also transitioned me into a different level of my faith.

Download your own personal FREE scripture meditation booklet here or send us an email:

melvinaministry@gmail.com

https://documentcloud.adobe.com/link/track?uri=urn%3Aaaid%3Ascds%3AUS%3A7bcdbb72-f1c8-4b89-9032-7e7c5cb6d860

Chapter Seven
Daring Faith

"This girl is not dead, she is only asleep," Jesus said. The Bible pronounces that the people who were there laughed scornfully at Jesus (see Mark 4). They made fun and a mockery of Jesus, the same Jesus they walked miles to see bringing their sick for healing. Jesus did not take offense! The people who do not understand your assignment and have nothing better to do; their own lives do not show any accomplishments are the ones who will stand to ridicule you and question your calling. The people saw what they wanted to see, the negative and the dead and they judged Jesus because He saw what they could not see. Have they ever laughed at your vision when you shared with them what God had told you? They gave you their impressive advice based on what they could see. Have they ever alleged that you were silly for dreaming such expressive dreams and going after what you believed in? They told you to be realistic and get a real job, stop dreaming and chuckled and made fun of you?

They don't have to believe your vision, if you believe what God has told you and walk toward your goal, God will elevate you where they will see you and remember their words.

The Bible says in Mark 4, that Jesus healed two different people who had come from a totally different background but for the same purpose; they both wanted healing from Jesus regarding blood flow. One came to Jesus expecting Him to start the blood flow of their dead child, the other came with the hope that Jesus would stop her blood flow.

Jairus was an important man in the community, a wealthy mega church official, a man of high standards who people revered. He was the spiritual leader and supervisor of all activities held in the Synagogue. He came out to seek Jesus to heal his twelve-year-old daughter. He is the kind of guy who drove in classy cars, lived in a large mansion, had servants, a driver-bodyguard to drive him around, lived extravagantly. He had everything money could buy but his vast empire could not buy his daughter's health. His daughter was on the verge of dying and his entire wealth and ministry could not save his little girls life because he lacked in one thing that activated the Heavenly resources, faith!

Now there was another person who did not have a fancy car, she walked miles with shoes that had holes underneath. She had to take it off several times to get rid of pebbles that stuck in her shoes. She took numerous interruptions from her walking to catch her breath as she was weak from losing blood for many years. She looked for shady places to take brief rests before she continued her journey toward her mission to find Jesus. Sometimes in life, we must take steps to where we want to go; start or invent something, do something because our answer will not come to us, we must go to it. Once we start where we are, the next phase reveals itself. Unless we change our mindset and decide that we want a change, the next step will make itself clear. The lady with the Alabaster Jar with a reputation and gossip behind her took bold steps to find Jesus as did this lady with the issue of blood; they both we unhappy with their current situations and *decided* to make a choice between life and death, to stay and accept their situation or step out in faith and find the resource that could help them get out. They did not wait for Jesus to come to them or send them help; they set out to find Him. Are you waiting for God to show up in your situation? What steps have you taken to find Him?

Even the wealthy leader Jairus who could have sent his servant to locate Jesus decided to go himself. He and his driver could have very well driven past this dirty looking peasant lady in their expensive car and did not look twice! She could have reached Jesus on time too if someone had given her a lift, but she could only walk as fast as her tired painful legs could carry her. She had been bleeding for twelve long years, in fact, her bleeding commenced the same time Jairus daughter was born. She was emaciated and ghostly looking, having lost a considerable amount of blood over the years. She was often tired, short of breath and thirsty with an irregular heartbeat. At times she had to stop and catch her breath as she felt dizzy. She fatigued easily and felt weak.

She did not live in a fancy large mansion, as the little she had she had spent it all on physicians. She did not have servants, she had no name as her name did not matter to anyone because she was a nobody. Have you ever felt like you did not matter to anyone, people overlooked you, and looked past you as if you did not exist?

Looking at the exterior, this woman had nothing in common with the rich leader Jairus, but life had placed them both in the same place, at the feet of Jesus, where they had something in common; they both had blood issues and they both needed healing.

Although in the ancient times births were at home with the midwives, however, let me escort you to the fake scene of what would have been if Jairus and the lady with the issue of blood were living amongst us now. Let us take a tour of the invented hospital where Jairus daughter was being born, a hospital for prestigious people, where the rich and affluent went for the delivery of their babies; a private hospital with the best of services, physicians who were imported from overseas with excellent credentials to perform best surgeries. The private rooms hosted large ensuites with pink and blue curtains and displayed tiny cribs lined up with matching pink and blue quilts. This private hospital's birthing unit was exclusive and exquisite.

Now walk with me to the public hospital across the road, further down, hidden behind the trees and shrubs for those who could not afford private medical insurance or pay for extra services. The poor and the needy came here to seek free or rather affordable medical assistance.

In the private suite of Jairus and his newborn child, a celebration had commenced with pink ribbons and balloons, greeting cards from their church members and well-wishers. There was much laughter and joy as well to do visitors arrived to see the newborn, bringing with them bouquets of flowers, gifts and chocolates. Pictures were taken and posted on social media, Jairus' name was hash tagging and trending as he was a well-known megachurch leader. In another room across the road, sitting alone was a disheveled looking lady with a haemorrhaging problem, sobbing hysterically, who had just received her diagnosis. One received happy news and is celebrating, while another received tragic news and could not stop crying. Little did they know that their paths would cross again in twelve years. People who had perhaps laughed at you because they thought they were better than you, rejected you because you did not have enough, you did not have the right skills or qualifications, right age or looks for the job, God is about to put you in a higher place than them, where they will notice you. Your paths will cross again with them, but you will be the one on top this time. Be like Joseph who said, "As for you, you meant evil against me, but God meant it for good", Genesis 50:20 ESV and forgive them because in your forgiveness is your power.

Being desperate can be a good thing

They both were desperate for the same thing. Do you know what desperate people are capable of doing? They don't care who is watching, they use everything they have to push through doors, they break all rules and boundaries to go after what they want. When they start to see in their mind where they want to be, their vision becomes bigger than their problem or what little they have in their hand. It becomes a force uncontainable and they become unstoppable. Whatever is fighting you, you have to win it in your mind first, and you do that by capturing each negative, disempowerment thought one at a time and replace it with what God has said in His word about that situation. For that, you need to read His Word and get to know Him personally, His will for you and His love for you. In His Word, you will find out what He has given you already, and once you let it sink deep down inside of you, it will set you free.

Jairus was desperate to get to Jesus quickly as He had no one else who could help his dying child. She was on the threshold of death and his chauffeur drove him in his fastest car to see Jesus who was his only hope. He was a powerful man, yet he did not hesitate to beg for his daughter's life. All the best physicians his money could purchase failed to help his daughter. The Bible mentions that there was a crowd of people, so there was a lot of pushing and shoving as people were bringing their sick to Jesus. Jairus was in a rush, he had an emergency. Have you ever had a critical situation where you needed God's help immediately or you would suffer a great loss, perhaps a diagnosis where doctors had given you limited time to live, a disease that was becoming worse, money for your rent was due and you had not been able to gather enough funds for, your house was about to be repossessed, you needed God critically to turn up, but God seemed to be too busy helping other people?

The gleaming car suddenly halted and Jairus' driver-bodyguard rushed to the passenger side and with one sleek movement opened the car door. Jairus shiny designer pointed shoes landed on the muddy dusty ground as he got out of his car wearing a custom-tailored suit. A whiff of his fragrance floated in the air. He strode toward the crowd to locate Jesus with his driver-bodyguard close beside him. The crowd was heavy, and the noise was deafening.

Finally, they located Jesus and requested Jesus to attend to his daughter for healing to which Jesus agreed. Jairus was rushing to get Jesus back to his daughter, as the Bible says she was on the verge of death and Jairus had no time to waste. It was a matter of life and death and Jairus could not afford the time to share Jesus with the crowd. Jesus followed Jairus; the crowd was forceful against them as they rushed to get out to the car. Jairus quickly looked behind to ensure Jesus was following him as he made his way toward his car through the multitude of people who were pushing and shoving. He reached his car and as he turned around, to his disappointment, Jesus was not there. He had lost Jesus in the crowd! Annoyed he looked at his driver-bodyguard and accused him of losing Jesus, *"How could you lose Him, what happened, where is Jesus, I told you to walk close?"* (Remember this is a fake scenario as if it was happening in our time). Jairus quickly glanced at his expensive gold watch and knew he did not have much time. He waved to his driver and together, they retraced their steps back into the crowd hastily, competing against the mass of people, to find Jesus. Finally, they spotted Him and raced to get to Him before they lost Him again. Jesus stood there speaking to the crowd, as if He had a moment of amnesia about His earlier appointment with Jairus. He was asking everyone in a loud manner, who had touched Him. Jairus was annoyed and restless, *"Jesus, hurry up, we don't have much time, my daughter could die any moment now, please! Of course, everyone is touching you, but never mind them, Jesus, we need to hurry please, c'mon, my daughter needs you."*

When we are very anxious and worried, pressed for time, other people's problems seem minor, our dire circumstances appear more important than theirs and we want Jesus to bypass them to come to us first. There were hundreds of people, the commotion was massive, and Jesus was asking who had touched Him. Hundreds of people had touched Him, prodded and pushed against Him but Jesus continued to ask relentlessly. It appeared like He was not prepared to leave till someone owned up. He kept looking for the person who had touched him with a purpose, not just a mere shoving. The Bible articulates that someone had received what they came for because virtue had gone out of Jesus. The lady with the issue of blood who had touched Jesus with determination was in all probability still nearby Jesus, trying to get away but due to the extensive crowd, she was not able to hurry. Trembling she came forward and told Jesus her entire story. We all know that if a woman starts to tell her whole story, it could take some time. While she was vocalizing to Jesus her entire life story, Jairus daughter had passed away. It appeared like one life had cost another life.

Jesus was too late; the time had lapsed for Jairus. His servant brought him the sad news of the demise of his child and told him not to bother Jesus, that it was too late. Imagine Jairus heart, being so close to the healer, yet not being able to get what He came for. Have you ever had something almost in your hand, you could feel it, smell it, but lost it in the last minute; perhaps that business deal or that job promotion, you yielded to the battle, succumbed to the failure, gave in to the divorce? Here was Jairus, who had struggled through the crowd to find Jesus, and was on his way to his daughter when out of nowhere someone else came in and took the healing that belonged to his daughter. He felt cheated, robbed, angry and resentful. Can you imagine Jairus muttering, *"Oh no! Not today Lady! You could have come any other day, why did you have to come today, the day I needed Jesus the most? Now you have messed up everything. This is not happening, you took my daughters healing. Jesus, how could you give my daughters healing to her, I got you first, I was here before her?"*

They meet again twelve years later, Jairus and this lady with the issue of blood, both with a similar problem. His daughter's blood had stopped flowing, she was dead, and this lady's blood would not stop flowing. Jesus *started* the girl's blood flow while *stopping* the lady's blood flow.

He is the author and finisher of our story!

Her blood was stopped, and another's was activated! Isn't it strange that the Mega church leader, the Synagogue official, who was in church all the time did not have faith like this lady who was poor and had a condition that did not even allow her to enter the synagogue?

We can be in church all week, wear our most expensive outfits and attend all the conferences, buy all the faith CDs, books and podcasts and do all our religious duties but still unable to activate our faith. All it took was her simple act of worship. She made her own strategy, thought of something others had not, her approach was radical. She declared to herself enough times that if she only touched Jesus, she would be healed. Her words embedded in her spirit and her mind and she started to believe what she was confessing. She could envision herself healed. She did not have to copy anyone else's style. She made her own method, her own style of worship. Sometimes we try hard to imitate someone we admire, but we have our own testimony to bring to God and that is enough to move His heart. God honors our faith even if it sounds strange and not how everyone else does it. God sees the heart, the persistent prayer of the righteous, the undefeatable faith, the kind of faith that can walk miles on bare feet in the heat of the sun, past all the bystanders, pushing through the crowd kind of faith that says no matter what the cost is, I will do it! I am sure in the crowd were hundreds of people who needed healing of some kind, but only one received it. Why is that, we read the same Bible, listen to the same worship and preaching but one goes away healed? It is that radical faith that rises on the inside, knowing deep down that Gods Word is final!

How often do we allow other people's own experiences of failure and scepticism speak into our destiny? We take their specimen and apply it to our situation and tell ourselves that it will not work for us because it did not work for them. Their destiny is not attached to you.

Just because your vision does not fit into their normal do it this way box, it does not mean there is anything wrong with it. Don't allow other people's disbelieve to hinder the process of your faith.

We all have had people in our lives or at work who have stated that they had always done it a certain way and refused to allow change. While the church official came to ask Jesus to visit his house to heal his dying daughter, here was a tiny lady who was not allowed in church but received her healing without Jesus visiting her home or praying for her. What an astounding act of faith of this underprivileged lady. She had no money, or status, she had no influence, nothing to bring to Jesus, except her simple childlike faith that said that even if she did not get to touch him in the crowd, just a touch of what he was wearing would be more than enough.

How badly do you want it?

I am reminded of another lady in the Bible with a supreme faith like this. In Matthew 15:27, was a lady who expressed to Jesus to allow her to assemble the crumbs that fell at the master table for her daughter's healing. Jesus was moved by her faith.

She was not a Jew, she was a Canaanite from pagan worshiping community, yet she came after the Jewish leader seeking mercy for her demon possessed child. Her plea was not answered by Jesus initially; He ignored her momentarily, but she was not moved by that. Sometimes it may seem like our plea is ignored, not answered but there is a reason for everything. She could have walked away empty and offended after Jesus called her a dog but because she was desperate for her daughter, she could not afford the luxury of taking offence. She was persistent in her ask. We need to be persistent in our request. Just because we prayed twice and our healing did not manifest, we give up saying it did not work!

She was a lady in distress. Her child needed healing and she was prepared to do whatever it took. She followed like a stalker wherever Jesus and His disciples went, calling out and begging loudly even when it annoyed the disciples. Isn't this the same thing that happened to Hannah in the temple in 1 Samuel 1? Hannah's prayer was also out of the ordinary that it annoyed the preacher who told her to be quiet, accused her of being drunk and making a showcase of herself. He told her to worship softly, not to show off. If you have not been violated, broken and despised like I have been, held your dying child, begged for bread, then you have no authority to tell me to worship softly, to be gentle because I have a praise stirring in my spirit. Because He found me in the pit, I bring to Him my best worship, my heart and my soul, so you don't tell me that my God deserves less, because I will shout, I will yell and dance till it breaks fear in my life, lifts the shame, breaks the chains, till demons flee.

You would imagine that these men of God would be understanding and helpful with a humble attitude, but these impetuous men came in the way of these ladies' miracles. They told Jesus to send her away, that she was too noisy. Be careful who you agree with when it comes to your calling or your healing; just because it did not work out for them, they might have the wrong intension about yours and speak negatively. If you listen to them, you will abandon your calling and walk away empty. Had these ladies listened to the church people, they would not have received their miracle.

Jairus daughter had no pulse, she was truly dead. It may have looked like Jesus was too late, but God has perfect timing for everything. He wants us to believe first. Everyone saw and knew that the girl was dead, but Jesus called her 'sleeping'. Jesus called the dead sleeping and while everyone mocked Jesus, Jesus did not care. He knew His word had power. It is not what it looks like, it is what the written Word says! God cannot lie, it is impossible for Him to lie. Whatever His word is spoken to, that object has to change to fit His Word. His Word will not bow, the entity has to bow. It is what He said that mattered, and not what it looked like or what others told Him. God has told us not to be moved by circumstances or how things looked like on the outside, but to trust Him.

This story teaches us many things; Jesus was there amidst a huge assembly of people, anyone could have received their healing, but they missed a great opportunity because they did not come hungry and desperate like this lady. How often we miss our chance of greatness by holding onto grudges, focusing our devotion on the trivial things from our past, and miss Jesus passing us by. This lady came from behind, unforeseen, who did not give up after many rejections. In the huge crowd, weak as she was from her disease, she was barely able to touch Jesus, but she settled for the tip of his garment, knowing that it was more than enough for what she came for. Because of the huge crowd shoving and pushing, she was only able to scarcely touch the tip of Jesus garment, giving herself permission for the transfer of healing virtue from Jesus to her, before the crowd thrust her over. The tiny touch was more than enough to heal her of the years of pain, loneliness, shame, and brokenness. Never underestimate people by beholding their peripheral appearances or their conditions. They might have more faith than you because

God does not see the exterior, He perceives the heart, He sees the faith. Jairus was the churchman, he could have asked Jesus to speak the Word and his daughter would have been healed instantly. He had the same measure of faith as this lady, but while his faith was lying inactive, this lady planted hers on a very rich soil and walked away with a miracle. We all are given the same amount of time, twenty-four hours and the same measure of faith, but some high achievers can accomplish more by capitalizing it.

Jairus' resume was impressive, he was brilliant in his job as the Church official and knew his religious obligations very well, but he lacked one very important skill; his ability to use his faith, unlike this lady who was considered unclean because of her bleeding and was not accepted in church, yet she showed a remarkable faith. She didn't care that she was not permitted in the church; she started her own church right there on the street where she worshiped Jesus unapologetically.

Sometimes while we are waiting for our miracle, it may seem like it went to someone else. While we are praying and still waiting for a husband, everyone else we know seem to be getting married, having their babies while we are still waiting to conceive, and God seems to have forgotten us and we lose hope. Although it seemed on the outside that it was too late for Jairus daughter, it is never too late. Everything is subject to change, nothing lasts forever! He is the Master of the storm. There is nothing too late for Him and no door He cannot open, but we must believe first. Faith requires a willingness to be inconvenienced so that we can re-invent ourselves as God sees us fit. Your greatness is in the first step you take out of your stagnant place.

Chapter Eight
Wilderness, the road to Destiny

The children of Israel had to go through a vast arid wasteland to get to their destiny. To get to the other side of our troubles, there are always some giants to slay, some mountains to climb, and some oceans to part. David was anointed to be a King when he was only a young boy tending to his father's sheep. He had the promise from God, but no crown and no palace yet. He did not know when or how he would become a King. Nothing in his life looked like he was the anointed King of Israel. He still worked for his father in the blazing heat and the winter cold days even when nothing looked like what God had promised him. God was preparing him to be a King right where he was, in his Sheppard job. I worked as a nurse and many times I held patients' hands and prayed while they passed on to the other side. Sometimes I was able to bring them to the Lord before they died, other times I just prayed. I did not know then that I was already in ministry. God uses us right where we are, but not always how we expect Him to.

Early one day David was asked to take his brothers some food (see 1 Samuel 17). God had a plan for David and was guiding his steps in the position where He could elevate him. While David was serving his brother's, God opened an opportunity for him to display in public what He had prepared in private. Everyone can dance, and raise their hands in church, but how is your worship when no one is watching, when tears fall down your cheek early hours of the morning, when what you have in your hand is not enough, are you still able to worship or are you complaining? David got recognized *after* he passed the test of killing the giant Goliath. Before God will elevate you, He will allow circumstances to filter you and when you do not succumb to the pressure, He will boost you up.

God might have spoken a word over you and you might still be out in the field with nothing in your life corresponding to what God has told you, but if you keep serving in the area He has called you to, be it in someone else's ministry, or helping in any capacity, God will open an opportunity for you right where you are. Always look for opportunities to influence someone, ways to add value to someone and while we are serving, God will allow us to be noticed.

Jesus the servant

Sometimes our blessing is hidden in the problem we are facing. David did not know that he would become famous when he left home to serve his brothers their meal. David did not know that God had a promotion waiting for him within the challenge he was about to face. God had the audience of the existing King to witness the rising of the new King. God will exalt you in the presence of your enemies.

God did not promise it was going to be easy, but He does promise never to leave or abandon us (see Deuteronomy 31:8). He has *allowed* that situation in your life so that you can see the *deliverance* of the Lord (Job). Without sickness, you cannot find healing, without trouble, you cannot find the promotion, without having a need, He cannot fill you. God lives in trouble; the Bible declares that He is a present help in times of trouble (see Psalm 46:1 KJV).

If you are in trouble; don't be afraid, because even though you may not see Him, He is right there beside you. Within your trouble is the breakthrough that is unseen to you, like a resting seed that has life concealed inside but only sprouts when placed in the right environment. Some circumstances in our life will cause our flesh to submit before we can experience a good thing to come out. I had to die to addictions, habits and fleshly desires in my life for the ministry and this book to come out. I did not know that my fragmented, messed up life was picked up by God to form a mosaic so beautiful. I love Mosaics because they remind me of how carefully God placed the shattered fragments of my life together.

God will take us through an extended way intentionally and permit adversities and conditions in our lives that may appear to break us, but He controls the intensity of those situations so that the perfect fragrance can be released. When we ask God to remove a trial that we are going through because it is difficult, and if He does, He will remove the whole lot, even the blessing attached to it. Like an antibiotic, finish the whole course so that you can reach the blessing that comes after the trial. Although the route might be long, unfamiliar and frustrating, but God will lead you to bring out resilience and the integrity required for the job.

When God sent me confirmations about my ministry through various people, I went through many emotions. I was older and I had no resources. I was to leave my secular job to go into a no job. I had a dependent family. Some enquired why interstate, surely if it was God, He could do it anywhere. I remember God had asked Abraham in the Bible to leave his family and everything he had known behind to go after his calling as his families were idol worshippers. God will move us to the right setting to position us to release our blessing. Moving interstate was no small task even for the young. My flesh took the better of me and I found myself pacing up and down in the small hours of the morning praying but also worrying. I knew worry is not from God and it is always associated with fear, but I indulged in it anyway. Just knowing the Word is not enough. It has to be actioned, spoken and believed by faith. When I was younger, I slept with the Bible under my pillow thinking it had the power to drive out demons and nightmares. For the Word of God to manifest in our lives, it has to be spoken and believed.

The enemy, satan will show you all the reasons why you should not and could not pursue something God had placed in your heart. Fear, if given a chance, would paralyse you and keep you worried which brings anxiety and palpitations and other physical manifestations of sickness.

Your emptiness is just the right ingredient for God

Moses had shortcomings like any one of us, yet God used him to bring out an entire nation to freedom.

I asked the Lord numerous times if He was sure about sending me. I could identify with Moses, because I too asked God similar things, how, why, but Lord, how could this be like Mary the mother of Jesus asked because I was the last person God could have called; broken, full of mistakes, no confidence, confused, lonely and full of guilt but God likes to use the least expected. Isaiah 14: 27 reads, "For the LORD of hosts has purposed, and who will annul it? His hand is stretched out, and who will turn it back?"

Many times, we look at the little in our hands and become fearful of doing the big things God has called us to do, just like the disciples of Jesus with the two fish and five loaves of bread in front of thousands of hungry people (see Matt 14). God told Moses to use that which was in his hand (Exodus see 4:2), and what Moses had in his hand was only a regular cane, a stick. God can only multiply and grow when we step out in faith and start where we are. I have often cried to Him about my inadequacies, that maybe He made a mistake when He called me. I told God that no one would want to listen to me, and I had nothing important to say, I was a nobody, I do not have a mega preacher father who could endorse me. How often we talk ourselves out of Gods purpose for our lives by listening to the doubts and lies of satan in our mind.

When we say these types of negative things as I did, 'that I am a nobody", it grieves God's spirit because we are made in His image and we are people made to carry His will, called into destiny with a purpose.

If God has placed something in your spirit that has been tugging at your heart strings and will not go away, and the enemy is telling you that you do not have the right skills, qualifications or the resources to do it, push yourself and do it anyway by faith.

God will ask you to do something huge, and then expect you to trust Him and do it by faith alone. He is the way maker, the provider, the limitless God. He will never ask you to do something that you can do very easily. He will always ask you to do something that you cannot do without His help. I could not stand in front of people and talk, I had stage fright. I told God, "What if I opened my mouth and nothing came out? Besides no one would invite me to speak anyway, as nobody knows me." We complain a lot rather than just taking God at His word. God has more ways to bless us than we can count. His ways are above our understanding. He is not asking us to work things out in our mind how God will do it, but to believe by faith. It was easier for me to believe when I was little because then I did not try to figure God out.

The first-time God surprised me, I will never forget was when I got off the train around seven in the morning and crossed the road to wait for the train in Richmond, Melbourne. It was a cold winter morning. I was draped in many layers of clothing. I could feel my toes curl with numbness inside my double layered socks within my boots. I had a phone call from my pastor who invited me to speak in a lady's conference that she was hosting. I was totally surprised as I had just relocated from interstate and barely knew her. What someone had prophesied about me was coming to pass. I understood than why God had led us interstate. The Lord was bringing me from the back to the front. I told her I was honored and accepted the invitation but as soon as I hung up the phone, the devil whispered to me that I should not and could not do it. He reminded me of my weakness, my stage fright and that I would make a fool of myself.

Momentarily I believed him. I rang my husband and told him about the invitation and he rejoiced and praised God and encouraged me but secretly, I was fearful. I had prayed, fasted, crawled, cried, sacrificed for my vision and when the time came for my day to preach, I panicked and nearly gave up my chance.

It took everything in me to encourage myself in the Lord till the time came for me to preach. I wanted to ring and make some excuse for why I could not do it. The devil will pull you down and tell you all the lies why it was impossible, why you could not do it, but you have to rise above it and say as Jesus did, "It is written," "I can do all things through him who strengthens me," (Philippians 4: 13 ESV).

I prayed most of the night for God to give me strength and that morning as I took the microphone with a trembling hand, my heart was racing with fear. I stood behind the pulpit and opened my mouth to speak my first public sermon in a church full of people looking at me. I wanted to throw the microphone down and run toward the door.

My speech was not of the learned and neither was it of a confident speaker, but I obeyed God and did what He asked me to do with fear and trembling. I delivered the message, but straight after that, the enemy laughed at my face telling me how bad my preaching was. I fought each thought the whole week and later found out that many people were blessed with the message I had delivered that day and received another invitation to preach again. God is so kind, He led me to 1 Corinthians 2: 1 to encourage me with Pauls experience as Paul narrates it, "When I came to you my friends, to preach God's secret truth, I did not use big words and great learning. For while I was with you, I made up my mind to forget everything except Jesus Christ and especially his death on the cross. So when I came to you, I was weak and trembled all over with fear, and my teaching and message were not delivered with skilful words of human wisdom, but with convincing proof of the power of God's Spirit. Your faith then, does not rest on human wisdom but on God's power."

I cried when God spoke to me through this scripture because I too spoke with a trembling voice and not with the eloquence of other big-time preachers and there was no loud clapping, but I took the courage to fight my fear and looked at the devil right in the eye and preached anyway. I was encouraged that Paul who wrote the New Testament, felt so inadequate like me.

Had I not taken the step forward into my destiny that day and allowed fear to rob me of the opportunity God gave me, those people would not have received the message God had for them that day. Everything in my life, my pain, my suffering and my losses had prepared me for a time like that, and I nearly allowed the enemy to steal it from me. The devil is a liar! The Bible says that obedience is better than sacrifice (see 1Samuel 15:22). It is okay to feel the fear, but necessary to do it irrespective of how we feel, move forward anyway, like I did and like Paul did. Goliath was huge and threatening, and David was a young boy who I am sure felt some fear and trepidation, but He encouraged himself in the Lord and fear or not, he moved forward and where God is there is liberty.

Prepare in your downtime

My opportunity to preach did not come easy. It took fifty years of training, of pain, shame, and suffering to break my Alabaster Jar and bring out the perfume that ministered to many that day. After that God opened many other doors and each time, I relied on Him.

When our calling heralds us, we will have no time to prepare, and that is why we need to prepare in our downtime while we are waiting for that invitation, for that business call because when it does come, we will not have any time to prepare. Most of us look at our down time as if it is permanent. Down time is the time when nothing seems to be working in our life. It's a misfit time. You may have fasted and seems to shift. It may feel like God has forgotten you. Downtime is usually the time when God is quiet like a teacher is during the exam time. You may be going through some difficult circumstances, and need God desperately to answer your prayer, but He does not say a word. Don't lose hope because every believer goes through a down time, a season of transition, a place where God is doing some work in you so that when the right time comes, you will present well before your goliath. When God directs that person to launch you, or that sudden invitation to speak in a church service, or that job promotion, or whatever you have in your heart, will you be ready? You prayed and fasted for it, but if you did not prepare mentally and emotionally, you will not be able to handle the breakthrough and the criticism that comes with reaching new heights with its new challenges. We never really arrive, we keep walking, it is all a journey, no destination.

I have books of sermons ready, as God was giving me sermon after sermon. It was a season of preparation as I was studying the word and listening to preaching to prepare myself, God started speaking to me about various things. I wrote in the early dawns and late nights, I wrote, and I wrote, I was ready and bursting, but I had nowhere to preach. I preached alone in my living room. It seemed like I was on fire. Preaching was coming out of me like water breaking forth. I could not sleep. Sometimes my husband was my only congregation or the birds and the trees outside. I preached to anyone and everyone who had time to listen. Even though I knew when the time came God would give me a right message for the right audience, but I kept writing, I kept preparing. I knew that day was approaching when God would say go!

While you are waiting, the enemy will come like a flood in various ways and challenge you through your loved ones, your families, your work, he will want us to mumble and complain, or give up because he knows your weakness and he knows very well what he needs to do to get you off the track. He knows he can distract you from your promise by getting your focus away to fear and anxiety and to gossip.

But the Lord says having done all, stand and see the salvation of the Lord. Open your eyes and appreciate the many little blessings along the way. In the Bible, the wheat and the weed grew together (see Matthew 23:25).

If you did not look carefully you would think it was all weed. Problems have a blessing hidden in them and if we are not careful, we can lose our blessing by mumbling about our problem. If you pulled one out, you risked pulling the other. Keep your eyes open and see the little victories along the way and as you keep giving God glory you will see the bigger victories. Worry and anxiety will rob you of your health. Just like you would toss a lolly to someone, toss your concerns to God. He specializes in troubles and hardships. He has the resources and the right people for you.

In Philippians 4:6 ESV, it says, "Do not be anxious about anything, but in everything by prayer and supplication with thanksgiving let your requests be made known to God."

Tell God your requests like you would in a shop. You take your requests, you give money and you walk away with your goods. In this case, the money exchanged occurred in the form of Blood and faith is the transaction currency. All you have to do is to put your requests direct line to God. He knows all forms of media and technology and walk away assured that delivery is guaranteed.

You are unique

There are some things God has called us to do that only we can do, and if someone else tried to imitate us, they would not be able to get the same outcome. God has our name written on gifts and callings. Our calling usually comes naturally to us, be it singing, playing an instrument, computer applications, cooking, something that we are passionate about, something that people can't talk us out of it? Don't ignore it, explore it. Don't worry about another person's calling or gift because you have your very own special gift that no one else can do but you. God has allocated a set audience for your speciality.

I set out to move interstate with nothing but a promise in my belly. I asked God for confirmation and it flooded with even strangers telling me that I was moving. I was apprehensive in taking such a huge step in faith. Even with God confirming, I was still 'secretly' uncertain and worrying. He did not give me anything, just a promise of the ministry, the promise of four hundred souls a week and directed me toward another city. This was our second huge move. We moved twelve years ago prior and that was when everything in my life changed, a bit like Moses, from the palace to the desert land, to finding my calling in the desert. Nothing in my life at that time showed any signs of Gods promise of the ministry but we kept digging like Isaac dug his father's old wells (see Genesis 26: 18). We kept pushing and declaring Gods promise like Abraham did and then I got my first invitation to preach. I started where I was, and God revealed the next step. I planted the little I had, and God increased it. When you are faithful with the little, He has trusted you, He will double the portion.

What have you got in your hand right now? Is it just a little bit of singing skills, or a tiny bit of dancing skills, some computer skills, good in math; use that little He has given you, and God will honor His word and grow it? Whatever your movement is, it could be a shift in jobs or anything that is causing you uncertainty, enquire of the Lord, don't wait till you have the resources or the perfect time, plant your little seed in someone else's life or ministry and God will stretch it. You will feel like quitting, the devil will tell you that you are not suitable for the job, you have no skills, no backup plan, that you are a failure before you have even started but when you make a decision, God will do it to prove that He is God. He will use your nothing to turn into something.

He is the potter, He knows how to mould the clay into something beautiful and He will do mighty things with your little, just trust Him.

God's Training School

Keeping up our faith and trust in God through the dark rocky places is not an easy task. When we have more bills than money, when we cannot fully provide for our family when they tell us that they will have to remove a breast because of cancer cells, when we have held our loved one in our arms as they took their last breath, and when we have lost everything we held close to our heart, then like Naomi in the Book of Ruth, we too will feel bitter and burnt, broken and empty. God reminds us in John 14:1-6 ESV, "Let not your hearts be troubled," because God knows exactly how our situation will turn out.

Face your situation head-on because God is with you. When I was contemplating to take my own life and that of my children's, God literally came for me. A small bible fell on my head as I reached out to the shelf above. I picked it up and opened it for the first time in seven years that I was in my wilderness. I opened the book of Psalms at the back and started reading. Straight away the spoken Word started to set me free. Sitting on the floor holding my two babies, I sobbed and repented and within days God moved mightily in my life and took me out of my situation and united me to my mother in Australia. When I strained to exit from my hopeless situation in my own strength, I kept going back to my past but when God moved in my life, nothing could stop Him. Even the immigration had no power over my mighty God of Israel because He opened doors for me that man could not open and He shut doors that I could not return to. He is powerful, and He does not forget you. He came for me and He will come for you too. It does not matter how bad your situation appears, or how profoundly addicted you are to illicit substances and alcohol, the Bible says that God's hand is not short that He cannot reach us, neither is He deaf that He cannot hear us (see Isaiah 59:1).

He remains God in bad times and in good times. Seasons change but He does not change. He is the same God who took the children of Israel out yesterday, and He still does miracles today. His resources are not controlled by the economy or inflation. When our enemies were aggressively chasing us, God was building us up. Their taunting, their harsh words, and abuses are empty words that will only return to them like a boomerang. It was the insults of the other woman that brought Hannah to her knees before God (see 1 Samuel 1). Her enemy did more for her than her friends because only then she was pushed to give God her crazy worship. Only when the olive is beaten and crushed, the pure oil comes out. Sometimes we are not able to see the blessing that is in our problems and our praises go to the enemy when we murmur. All we see is the huge boulder in front of us and we panic. We forget that God is the rock of ages, even the rocks will praise Him if we are silent (see Luke 19:40). Even the ocean waves had to listen to the command of God and rolled up its sleeves for the children of Israel to cross over to the other side. He knows what is in your bank account and He sees the bills stuck on your fridge door. He knows your heart before you even utter a word.

David was a powerful king and reigned for many years. His fame reached far and wide, but his humble internship commenced initially tending to his father's sheep out in the fields. Each fight he had with the predators to protect the sheep gave him a new set of skills and taught him flexibility. Perhaps for a period initially there could have been a possibility that he was terrified of the lions and bear that came for the sheep but ultimately as he advanced in his skills, he overcame his fear. When faced with the giant Goliath, David used the same principle, the same skill he acquired in the fields to fight anything that threatened the sheep in his care.

His resume described his well-developed skills and experiences in fighting the intimidating and aggressive adversaries. He was convincing in his pitch to the king about his warrior capabilities. When King Saul offered him a specialized outfit for his contest, David declined because he preferred to use what he was accustomed to.

Here are six helpful suggestions to fight the Goliaths in our lives;

1. **Be confident in yourself.**
2. **Fight with the tools that has been tried and proven.**
3. **Be your authentic self.**
4. **Know who you are and who has your back.**
5. **Do not doubt.**
6. **Do not be afraid.**

Our ability to contest in a battle is enhanced when we fight with verified tools that have been tried successfully previously. Our unique skills might be peculiar to others but when placed under Gods anointing, we will triumph. Many of us have overcome massive battles in our lives, some lost their homes and loved ones, their livelihood, but we survived to tell our story. The same weapons we used to fight those battles are available to us today. Deep down inside of us, we still have that fire burning, the fire of the Holy Spirit. We need to fan that fire, arise in our spirit and charge at the enemy who has been stealing from us. For too long we have kept quiet. The time has come when we need to arise in holy indignation and say to the devil, "Enough, you will not take from me, because it is written that when the enemy is caught, he must pay sevenfold," (See Proverbs 6:31)

We are spiritual warriors, God has prepared us for battle, and we should be equipped and ready every day.

To fight spiritual battles, we need to meditate on the scriptures and declare it each time the enemy brings in bad news or a sickness. You may not see any immediate alteration and the enemy might even laugh at you, but you need to keep speaking it loud till that problem bows to the Word.

The Word of God says in Isaiah 55:11, that Gods word does not go back to Him without doing what it was sent to do. If it was sent to heal, it must heal. The Word of

God once spoken out releases faith and the Word will manifest.

We cannot give up easily just because it appears insurmountable from the exterior. The word of God articulates that we should fight a good fight of faith, which means till the end, not giving up in the middle when the pressure is high (see 1 Timothy 6:12).

The Bible says David did not give up easily when things went bad in his life. We can always trace his steps leading back to God, worshiping somewhere.

David at Ziklag running away from Saul ended up in huge strife (1 Samuel 30). The Bible narrates that he and his men returned from a battle and instead of being welcomed by their families to celebrate their victory; they realized that the enemy had captured everyone and set the town on fire.

How do you think David and his men felt, coming home tired, finding their town on fire and everyone gone?

His men turned against him. The Bible says that David was deeply distressed, and he encouraged himself in the Lord by recalling the mighty hand of God in his life in his many previous battles. David felt the emotions any man would feel in a situation like that, sad, beaten and downcast but he reminded himself of how good God had been to him in the past. He was an influential king, but when it came to his relationship with God, he was always humble. He recognized that the only way to Gods heart was through worship. He opened his heart to God, bragging on Him, praising Him and seeking His advice about everything in his life and that pleased God.

How many of us turn to worship when our hearts are bleeding, when the physician pronounces bad news, or when our manager calls us to the office and tells us that our contract has been terminated? We go straight to the phone and ring a friend or family and tell them the bad news and talk for hours discussing the bad manager and how unfair they have been to us. Not everyone can deal with our nakedness when we tell them our deep dark secrets. David went straight to God and with God by his side, he marched to the enemy's backyard and took by force all that they took from him and much more. That is how good our God is that he restores seven-fold (Proverbs 6:31), much more than we have lost.

Whatever is keeping us awake at night, causing us to pace the floor and worry, be it sickness, or our children, or addictions, loss of job or marriage; you cannot give up without a fight. Start telling God how good He has been to you, providing for you, and remind yourself of His goodness and mercy and see the power of God come into your situation.

For many years I was suffocating under the piles of my own rubbles of shame and solitary, not being able to trust anyone or confide my heart to anybody. They say a woman's heart is like an ocean, deep with secrets. God began to shovel layer by layer of insecurities, shame, disappointments, heartaches, and pain. One day I realized I was no longer the same person I used to be. God had performed an emotional surgery in me by getting rid of parts that were diseased with emotional hurts and bitterness. God utilizes situations and disappointments in our life to train and prepare us for His best. We may not comprehend at the time and may desire to exit our troubled waters in haste, but we cannot abort the test till we pass, otherwise we may have to partake it again till we are permitted to get to the next level, because God loves us too much to leave us in our mess. His mercy is everlasting even when He is training us in the broken places of our lives.

Chapter Nine
Transition

People may share their wonderful testimonies about the goodness of God in their lives, how He gave them victory over their enemies and their addictions and gave them the desires of their heart, but no one tells us about the 'waiting' time, the part where they had to stand in faith even when nothing was shifting in their lives. They converse about a shift in their circumstances, that God made a away for them, a sudden change that transformed their lives, a place of worship where God met them and brought them out, but they don't show us their scar. There tell us the beginning and the end, but the middle part is the part where they don't tell us. The part where you don't want tomorrow to come, where you begin to doubt your calling; that is the part when nothing in our lives shows that

God is in control. The painful waiting part that no one talks about, where your bills pile up like a rubble from a hurricane, where the cancer has spread in your body and you are waiting for your healing, when your income stream has dried up, when your spouse has walked out on you leaving behind a debt you cannot pay, and when all hell seems to have broken loose in your life, what do you do then? Days when you lie awake wondering if what God promised you in His word or a prophetic word would ever come to pass? Elizabeth in the Bible was in a transition from barrenness to life; she had the promise of God growing in her belly in her senior years, but the baby appeared dead inside her (Luke 1: 41). Imagine the thought that would have been going inside her head, the enemy's whispers that her promise was dead. Was she always full of faith, I don't think so! I am almost certain that like all of us, there would have been times in her life where she doubted God's promise because she could not feel the baby. She would have battled fear of losing the child they wanted so much. Coming so close to having a child and then losing it was unbearable. God gives us a promise and expects us to trust Him even when we cannot see any movement in our situation. This is the time when we must go in all the way with our faith even when we don't see any result and trust God completely without reservation. When we are in a tight place, a place of pressing, that is when we want to quit and go back to our old job or whatever we were doing when God found us, but God calls us to wait and be still. When you have buried your child, said goodbye to the love of your life for the last time, when you have sat alone having a chemo, when everything you have built is taken away, when your own turn against you, you will have moments of doubt about Gods promise. My child had died, my marriage was over, my dreams had deceased, I had no income, it was over for me, but it wasn't over for God, it was just the beginning because when we are empty, He is able to fill.

Transitions

People relocate a few times in their life and for various reasons; maybe a downsize after children have all left home or a change in jobs. Whatever the purpose may be, a move is merely saying farewell to that season in our life and welcoming a new season, a new chapter God has opened before us. Change ushers something new. It requires us to let go of the old. We cannot arrive at a place without exiting a place.

Apart from physical transitions, there is a spiritual transition; from one level of faith to another level. When we believe God for superior results, our faith must match that, it must be stretched even when we don't see immediate change. At one point, we might have had to believe for small things like shoes for our children, money for groceries and pay for bills and school fees. They were the big things in our life. But after we fought some giants and shed some tears, our faith was amplified to a higher level where we required additional faith. Some things take an extended time to manifest as other people might be involved in our breakthrough.

The same principle applies as our need's increase, our faith must increase and along with it our standing time. The bigger the demand is, the longer we must stand in faith. Change may not always come the way we expected it to come and sometimes we even miss it because of fear and lack of obedience. There are times when we get attached to our current circumstances and choose to stay in that situation, although we may be aware that it is not the place we want to be or is healthy for us, however, fear holds us back and keeps us bound. Most Christians will tell us to be content. Being content will make us settle for mediocre, for less than our potential, where we think, "At least I have a roof over my head, or at least a got a job."

He wants us to step out by faith and walk on the water.

I observe these things when I have a vision.

1. Think it & write it down.

2. Pray about it, ask if God is in it.

3. Look at it regularly/daily.

4. Visualise it/Imagine it in your mind

5. Believe it.

6. Speak it out loud.

Remember the Word (Jesus) became flesh; when our thoughts and what we say become real in our mind, it becomes flesh, takes form in the physical.

Look at the possibilities in God's hand. He is more than enough to take us from our nothingness to greatness.

Some of us have asked God to show us our purpose, we have prayed for our vision, but when God reveals it to us, we are too afraid to take that step into the promised land because the giants are too big, or our resources are too small. God wants to give us more than we expect, because our expectation is too small for His plan for our life. He has already told us that His thoughts and plans for our life are bigger than what we could imagine (see Jeremiah 29:11). He wants to prosper and help us succeed in every area of our life, but our small thinking keeps us behind the line of succession.

The enemy kept firing his strongest bullets to make me quit, doubt and question God, to weaken my stand in God but I was determined not to go back to where I was before. I wanted more for me. Our answer will not come easy, as he will try to block our paths and send our friends and families to pull us down and create division in our family. We cannot compromise with God, either we choose Him, or we don't, we cannot sit on the fence.

Satan will constantly target our will and emotions, our mind. He wants us to be confused about Gods plan for us. He will accuse us, will bring our past failures, causing guilt and shame. Some demons are from generations, we are fighting our grandparents' demons, demons that has been in the family for many years way before we were born. When we accept Jesus as our Lord and savior, it draws a blood line that these generational demons cannot cross.

Things that make us sluggish in our career, in our spiritual journey, in our finances, we must not accept but fight spiritually. Faith is a fight, prayer and fasting is a fight. This journey we are in is a contest, a race we are competing to win. We are fighting daily but not in the flesh and blood but spiritually. They will come but they will not win because we have the power in the spoken Word that comes out of our mouth from our belly; the Words we have put in. So, if we have not put in any Word of God in our heart, nothing can come out from the reserve, because the Word of God is alive and does what it has been sent to do. John 7:38 says that when we believe in God, out of us will flow living water, the kind that heals and gives life to dead situations.

I started talking to God when I was a child, I even fasted. No one asked me to, I just did. I gave offering in church even when I was little because my mum gave me and my siblings coins to plant in church. We didn't have much, but she taught us to give. I won the lottery when it came to my parents, because they gave me something money cannot buy, they gave me Jesus, my helper and my best friend.

The enemy had put many barriers in our lives once we *decided* to sell and move in obedience to God's purpose for our lives. Each step we took forward was met with roadblocks and setbacks, bringing us right back to where we started and sometimes even worse. It was enough to bring doubt, unrest, and confusion, but when we know who the author of doubt, confusion, and fear is in our lives, we can go ahead and fight with the Word of God.

When I fasted for forty days, literally all hell broke loose in my life. I mean four car accidents one after another, everything at home broke down, attacks on our bodies, on everything we owned, on our children, a real cyclone hit our house bringing down our fences on both sides. It was like the devil had sent the cyclone just to our house because he knew we were going on the other side of our season, we were stepping over into our destiny, just as he did in Mark 4: 33-41, when Jesus had *decided* to go on the *other side* and the enemy sent a storm suddenly in the middle of nowhere, without any forecast of a bad weather.

The scripture says, Jesus rebuked the storm, because it was no ordinary storm. Once we have made up our mind to get out of our situation, the devil will launch an attack to stop us from going to the other side.

The storm sent in my life was also no ordinary storm. It was a spiritual war, manifesting in the natural, on the body and possessions. He wasn't after my things; he was after my will, my promise, and my destiny. He knew if he tried to shake everything in my life, it would cause me confusion, doubt and I would give up on my calling.

The enemy's fury went on for a long season, and it was extremely difficult not to look at the flesh, as the intensity of the attacks launched in our lives increased but we were determined.

It is strategized to paralyse us in fear, enough to stop us from getting out and trying. It will not subside when we speak to it once, because it will test our faith and our stance in God. Most times I have stood and commanded the storm, real-life storm to be quiet and it would start to storm louder and rain harder to show me that what I said did not work, that Jesus Name did not work. I learnt to recognize the tactics of the enemy and knew it would eventually subside if I did not doubt, and it always died down after trying to scare me into giving up first.

Each time a huge attack came in my life, I would read the book of Job in the Bible and put my name over Job's name and imagined a dialog about me in Heaven between satan, and God, and that encouraged me. We lost much in those few years, but what we gained spiritually was far greater than what we lost. Our faith had arrived at a new level where we literally laughed each time bad news came announcing a loss or a diagnosis or some form of trouble that tried to steal our joy and focus from God.

When Jonah tried to run away from his calling to go to Nineveh, yes, Nineveh repented, and God forgave them, but at the same time, it was Jonah who was transformed as well (see Jonah). He saw firsthand the mercy of God. I also was a changed person, the troubles that came to shake me, instead made me stronger. I no longer enjoyed the company of people I used to enjoy, and things that held my interest in the past did not interest me any longer. The storms that came in my life changed me.

I was reminded of Esau (Genesis 25) who gave his birth-right of the first born away for a bowl of soup. I was ready to give my calling away, because I was afraid what would people say if I did not preach with the confidence of other big-time preachers and did not get enough 'Amen' and 'Praise the Lord'. I was looking on the outside, the fake exterior rather than God, and comparing myself to others, and in my mind, I did not measure up to their way of preaching and brought myself down. I had to find my own way, my sweep spot because like David, I could not wear someone else's suit. I had to change my mindset, my thought pattern in order to pursue my purpose.

If God asks you to do something you can do, why would you need faith? How would God be glorified if it was easy for us to do?

It was only when I stepped out in faith to be me, not anyone else; God was glorified because I knew I could not do it on my own.

Choose you this day who you will serve

Mary the mother of Jesus chose to believe the promise given to her, even though it seemed impossible for a single untouched girl to become pregnant. The lady with the issue of blood, daring to leave home that day, knowing it was going to be impossible in the crowd to touch Jesus, she took a chance anyway in faith. Moses was called to bring out the children of Israel, he feared to return to what broke him, but he went back anyway in faith trusting God.

The Bible says (Hebrews 11:1) that faith is the substance of things hoped for, are you hoping for things that you cannot do unless God intervened, because I know I am?

When we do things Gods way, it does not matter how tired we are, how less we have, God will always bless us with more than what we went in with. He says not to fear, only believe (Mark 5: 36; Luke 8:50).

Faith when planted, it grows and brings result. When I was little, it was easier to believe as I did not try to work God out, or how He was going to do it.

Faith does not have a time limit; however, it can be useless if it lies dormant like any seed. If planted in the right environment, it has the potential to grow and produce after its own kind. There is no big or small faith; it is how long we are prepared to stand.

One day I was rejoicing and thanking God for the four souls I had brought that week and suddenly I heard an impression in my heart, "Believe me for four hundred souls a week." I told God it was impossible. That bringing four souls a week was difficult enough, that I was not some mega preacher who could gather that many people in one meeting. I proceeded to write down what the Lord said in my special journal book, and I dated and timed it and then crossed it off and wrote forty souls a week. I told God to be realistic, that even forty was impossible for someone like me who did not have a congregation. I said to God, *"Look at me Lord; I am only a little Island village girl that people don't even know, and where would I go to bring that many souls in one week, 7 days Lord? Why would they want to listen to me, what do I have to say?"* I told myself that perhaps it wasn't the Lord, that it was just me.

I went about my way, and then I heard again, *"I told you to believe me for four hundred souls a week, not forty."*

I froze for a moment. I heard again. I repented straight away and went back and wrote a fresh new line of what the Lord had said. I can't bring four hundred people to the Lord, but He can. I was looking at my own ability and my own resources and it was impossible. He didn't ask me to do it; He said to 'believe' Him for it. When, where, and how, was His business. Since then my husband and I have been believing and declaring it and keeping it before our eyes. It has not come about yet, but we know it will, because when God said it, it will come to pass.

Although salvation is open to anyone, it will not come to you without your permission. Salvation is by choice just as healing is.

I once illustrated to a gentleman who was always asking me what the good God was doing in my life. He was a gentleman the Lord had placed across my path. I would tell him about the Lord, and he would happily listen and smile. Each time I would ask him if he wanted this Lord who I knew. He would politely say, "Not today Mel." I would show him this illustration, *"This is a glass of water, you can sit there thirsty and die of dehydration or pick it up and drink it, the choice was yours."* He would look amused and nod.

Weeks went by and I continued to minister to him. I was drawn to him. Each morning as I left my bag in my office, I made my way to his room where he resided in a senior home. He would patiently wait for me. If I did not go to visit him, he would send for me. He just loved to hear what God was doing in my life, my little testimonies.

One morning I did my usual round and went to his room. His bed was made up with fresh sheets and there was silence. He was gone, he has passed away. I walked to my office and sat down as tears rolled down my made-up face. I strangely missed my fellowship with him. I knew why the Lord was sending me to him every morning. I told the Lord that maybe I should have tried harder or said something different. I saw the love of God for this soul, that He would send someone over and over for months. The Lord whispered in my heart that it was his choice. He had decided He did not want salvation each time I asked him for weeks and months.

Salvation is open to anyone, and the choice is ours to accept Jesus as our Lord and Savior and live an abundant life. God does not force us. His love pulls us to Him because of His mercy. To become born again, we must first believe in our heart that He is Lord and ask Him into our heart as our Savior. He comes by **our** *permission,* **our** *choice.*

Same with healing, it is available to all, but to *become* healed you must have the *faith to receive it* by giving permission.

How do we get enough faith? How do we grow faith? The Bible says faith comes by hearing the Word of God (Romans 10:17). There was a time in my life, I carried my iPad even to the toilet, to the bathroom, as I was hanging washing, or in the gardens, to hear preaching. I knew I had to keep listening to grow my faith, otherwise, I would have drowned under the stress that was placed on me at that time.

I listen to preaching when I am doing the dishes, when getting dressed and even when I am driving, it builds me up so that situations cannot pull me down.

If I am not listening to a faith preaching, then the devil starts putting thoughts in my mind about impossibilities in my life, and I would rather not hear his lies. I cannot rely on just Sunday worship and the church, I need to be plugged into the Word daily, as I cannot function as a wife, as a mother, as a friend without the Word. It is nourishment to my soul. It is the mirror where I see myself daily. It changes me to be the person God has made me to be.

We are very blessed to have YouTube and other forms of social media where we can hear preaching and teaching online without any cost; and there is no excuse why our faith cannot grow. We can't always rely on the church alone to teach us; we should have a hunger enough for the Lord to search for Him ourselves, to want to grow outside of church when no one is looking. It is our own responsibility to develop an intimate relationship with God. We cannot keep running to the pastor each time we have a situation. We should be able to lay our hand on ourselves and pray and cry and claim our healing. We don't need to go to a priest to declare our sins; we have our very own high priest, Jesus who pleads with the Heavenly Father daily on our behalf. The Holy Spirit resides in us helping us daily in all our situations, giving us reassurance that we are never alone.

Chapter Ten
When God Calls You, Get Ready for a Fight

We can call ourselves Christians but still have difficulty believing God to be our provider, our healer, our friend who cares for us. We get an instant high when we hear powerful faith sermons in conferences but when we come home to one big wave of issues, we hit rock bottom again. To keep in the Word right throughout the week, helps us stay focussed on Him and not on the circumstances around us. We can hear all the preaching we like and attend great church conferences and keep our purple colour fragrance journal, but if we do not practice it, and learn to pray and trust Him through our own issues, and exercise our own faith, and then we will be an ineffective Christian.

The intimacy is between us and God, and we are the only one who can spend that quiet time with God, nourishing the relationship. The doctor can prescribe medications, but if we don't take it, we cannot get it to work. Each time Jesus told the people who came to him for healing, that *their* faith had made them whole. Their faith drew virtue out of Jesus. It cost Jesus His life, it will cost you faith to receive healing.

The Word of God is the medication prescribed by the Doctor Jesus, for us to take as many times for it to work in our organs, body systems, and processes. His Word is alive and active, it cuts through bones and marrows, fixing all that needs fixing (Hebrews 4: 12). The Bible says it is sharper than a two-edged sword, penetrating even to the dividing soul and spirit. Nothing is as sharp, as transparent and as powerful as the Word of God.

We allow our hearts to worry about things that God has already taken care of. I used to worry and lose my appetite, even though I said I trusted God, I thought I could secretly worry. When troubles come, don't stress, worship God. I know it sounds strange when your entire life begins to fall apart, and God is saying to worship Him. Because He perceives the end from the beginning, He knows what is ahead of us. I express this to myself quite often and talk to myself with encouraging words.

The Word of God says He listens to the broken heart and the contrite spirit He will not dismiss (Psalm 51: 17). He sees our tears before they fall, He sees our hearts that is why when we complain about someone to God who has wronged us, God sees their heart and not so much as the wrong they did. They probably made it right with God.

We see the outside and judge, but we don't know the real story or their relationship with God, so it is best to mind our own business and pray for them without judging. Let God do His business.

Our calling always involves people because Jesus died for people. We cannot love Jesus and hate people. The church is the hospital of God full of the sick, addicted, broken people. We cannot turn people away by our attitudes and behaviors because they may look and act different to our beliefs.

You have a destiny and where you are in the present time, is not where you are supposed to stay. You are just passing by, so learn not to be so serious, sit back, worship God, sing His praises and let Him fight His own battle (2 Chronicles 20:15).

I had a sudden elbow pain. It just came without any exertion and it lingered for months. I kept confessing healing over it, and it seemed to have worsened. Months went by and I kept talking to it. One day I realized the pain was not there. It is not that my healing did not come when I prayed and believed the first time. Healing was already mine because Jesus had already paid the price for it. We give up saying, the prayer did not work. Have you heard people say, "I have prayed and fasted, but it is not working, nothing is happening?" They have just prophesied that nothing is happening, so they receive what they have declared.

Let the oil run over

Jesus' cousin was sitting in the Jordon and Jesus asked to be baptized by him. John did not feel that he had what it took to baptize Jesus the Messiah. After Jesus is baptized, Jesus is announced by God (a voice is heard from Heaven). Jesus who was already anointed in the womb was kept hidden till He was announced after His baptism. God may anoint you but keep you hidden till it was time to expose you. It is already in you, you are not waiting for it, but God is drawing things out of you to ensure you are ready to face the challenges of your calling when He finally broadcasts you. Anointing requires us to go through a process of filtering to certify us with what it takes to do all that God has called us to do. If you have been waiting for some time for your calling to manifest, God is about to pull the curtain on you. He will elevate and herald you in public but remember soon after Jesus was announced He was also led by the Spirit in the wilderness to be tested of the devil. That is what God was formulating in you, equipping you to embrace the challenges of being His hands and feet in the public eye. When that time arrives, Heavens will come down to celebrate you but also the spirit will lead you to be tested of the devil. That is why God has been preparing you so that when you are being tested and tried, you will be ready for it and not quit. Moses was called early but announced much later in his life. That was why nothing in the river could harm him as a baby because of his anointing. Your enemies will try but will not be able to touch you because of your anointing.

Not everyone will understand what it takes to be called, anointed of God with a mission and be there to encourage us when we are being tested and tried, when the debtors are knocking on our door, but they will be in a haste to pull us down and laugh behind our back. In 2 Kings 4:1, a widow of a prophet was in trouble with her husband's debtors who displayed no mercy in demanding their money back. They threatened to take her sons to be their slaves until the amount was paid off. We all have had experiences with merciless debtors in our lives, who were quick to throw us on the street when our payment was overdue by even a few hours. When I read the scripture, I wondered where were her friends, all those people her husband had ministered to? When all is going well in our lives, we have many friends who call us for coffees, movies, long chats but when all is lost, when we can no longer afford the coffees and movies, when our purse is empty, and the petrol tank is running on red light, they stop calling us? They don't return the money they owe us and block us on all social media and phone. Slowly we fall off their radar. But Jesus never shuts His door on us. When He hung on that cross of Calvary, Jesus at some point became you and me with all our lack, sins and diseases. No one can understand us better than Him.

When He announces you, the enemy cannot stop you; your destiny has been set already when you were conceived in your mother's womb.

Chapter Eleven
Fear is a thief

Fear is the killer of faith. Fear works opposite of faith. Just as faith pleases God, fear pleases the devil. Faith activates good things in our lives, fear activates bad things. Faith breaks chains and sets us free, fear bounds and holds us back. Faith is Gods tool, fear is devils' tool. The battle about us is between God and Satan. And the battle is the Lords. Every negative thought that comes in our mind will lead us to fear and worry.

I had trust issues and was highly suspicious because of my past circumstances in my life. The devil will always bring our past in our present relationships. He will tell us that we have been a failure in the past. I praise God that He has restored me. Negative thoughts, jealousy, and anxiety will come back repeatedly; we must learn to cast it out again and again until it shuts up. If we look at our lives now, it's mostly the result of either good or bad choices we made in the past. Everything we are doing today is the result of taking a risk to step out in faith and obey God in our past. Getting married, getting pregnant, buying a home, taking that job, or that study, it has all been a risk of faith.

The ammunition the enemy sends is more powerful ones each time because you are a step higher in faith. Don't fear, his attacks will not last. You may have to stand longer, while the heat is hotter.

In the book of Joshua in the Bible, God told Joshua who was the team leader ushering the people of Israel into the Promised Land which God had **given** to them, but they did not have it yet, although it was given to them. They had to go and possess what was already theirs. I can post you a gift that I bought for you, it is yours, I have posted it already, but you have not received it yet, but it is yours.

Standing is difficult when we are weak from fighting and are exhausted; that is when the devil hits us the hardest. We see loss and brokenness all around us and no victories from our efforts, but God has said that when we are weak, His strength is made perfect in our weakness (see 2 Corinthians 12:9).

In the Bible, Jesus' cousin, John the Baptist was locked up in jail, feeling helpless during his adversity, he doubts about Jesus being the Messiah (Matthew 11:2), and asks if Jesus was for real. When we have found ourselves in dire circumstances, we all have at some point doubted God, if He was real why wasn't He showing up in our situation?

Sometimes it is not so much about the victory, it is the process that changes us, builds us and helps us to expand in our territory.

We look at the children of Israel and often wonder why meandered in the desert for forty years when their journey could have ended sooner but aren't, we all been wondering in our desert for a long time, (see Joshua 5:6). We may not be wandering lost in the real desert but all of us have, or are still wandering in our life deserts, in our addictions, in our pasts, in our "what ifs" and what could have been, and our sorrows of what might have been and in our unforgiveness.

Some of us carry a grudge for years and have been struggling with that toxic relationship or binge drinking or some other form of strong-hold in our life, walking through the same road over and over for many years and getting nowhere. Life does not discriminate anyone.

We are no different to the children of Israel in many ways. We are also wandering in the desert, except not on foot but in our mind and our thoughts. Each year we are in the same fight.

The children of Israel were surrounded by their enemies in the desert and they feared being caught and taken back. Have you ever felt like a failure, that your enemies had won? You fix this situation here and that one breaks over there, you take two steps forward and five backwards, and you ask God why? All the while the enemy laughs, *"Where is your God now?"* (Psalm 42:3)

I doubted my own ability, and that God would even look at me twice, let alone pick me to preach to bring the good news to someone. The calling was very big, in fact, God called it 'mammoth' and when I saw what I had in my hand and what God had asked of me, it scared me. I ran and did not accept it. I found jobs that I was not happy in but God in His mercy, used me even in those jobs to bring souls to Him one at a time. Like David, God used my jobs to train me. Little did I know that I was on Gods training school when I sat with a dying people holding their hand and gently bringing them to the Lord as they passed on, or that person in the train to work or that individual in the staff room going through a painful divorce. I was everywhere God wanted me to be. I would be assigned to a job for a few months, or a year or two and move on and wondered why I was not like other people who kept the same job for twenty or more years. I was searching for something but not sure what I was searching for. In my jobs, I often ministered to people. They would seek me out to talk to me about their issues or ask for prayer without me saying anything to them. I would stay in jobs and then move on like my time there was over.

Till later I started to see the pattern and could see how God was using me to bring good news to people through my jobs. He was using everything around me to teach and train me in my calling. I was evangelizing since as long as I can remember and throughout my life, still, I did not know that I was in my calling and they were my training years. It took me years, through many heartbreaks, lost opportunities, and God chasing after me to finally accept my calling.

And when I did, suddenly all hell broke loose in my life. No one ever teaches you what to expect in a transition, what to expect when calling calls? The disciples all left what they were doing, to follow Jesus, was I meant to drop everything I was doing to follow Gods plan for my life? I was too busy trying to work God out, how He was going to do it and most times I would be in fear. I would tell God why I could not do it. Why I was not a suitable candidate.

Everything started breaking in my life when I accepted Gods plan. Troubles of all kind landed at our doorstep, a bit like Job in the Bible and in the midst of rubbles God said, 'move forward.'

God says to take a step forward, to go ahead, fear or not keep moving. In Exodus 14: 13-14, Moses told the children of Israel not to be afraid, to stand by and see the salvation of the Lord. The enemies who are standing against you today, the Lord is saying you will not see them again because the Lord is removing them.

When the children of Israel moved forward, the ocean waves started to roll like a rug and pile up on the sides as they crossed the dry ocean bed. If they stood looking at their problems, listening to the steps of the enemy closing in on them, they would have been gripped by fear as it was a dead end. We often stand and look at the problem and talk about it to everyone who could not help us, except to God who could.

Months went by and I continued to work in the ministry God gave us by faith. I wrote sermons, fasted and prayed. I prepared the website and recorded podcasts and wrote blogs, but no movement of the baby. I continued to do all I could in faith. I studied the word and went for long prayer walks. I used that which I had in my hand and expected God to grow it as He had promised. Every day and night my husband and I declared Gods promise. I would tell him, I am in my office. I would get dressed as if

I was really going into the office. I took breaks like in the office and all the while the devil laughed on my face.

Each Friday, I would work on this book, and on the podcast, on the website and fast and pray. I did not pass my card to anyone or try to ask anyone to invite me, it was what God did.

You will not see the fruits unless you plant a seed, and while you wait for it to grow, you continue to water it with praises and weed it with worship and only then in its season, you will see the harvest. At times, like everyone else I also doubted and became frustrated, felt low in faith and asked God, how long and when? My husband, a man of God often encouraged me in the Lord. God also sent His Word in the timely manner to lift me up when I felt like I was sinking. We need each other.

But I also knew if I gave up, where would I go? I had already tried the world and did many jobs, ran away from my calling for so long and was not settled in anything

I had done. My calling kept tugging me and bringing me back, and I knew I could not be happy doing anything else but my calling.

My husband and I continued to seek God, kept declaring and prophesying what He had told us.

We made up our mind to keep going till we saw results, till all that He promised came to fruition and we refused to accept defeat. Be ready to stand no matter what.

Chapter Twelve
Jesus Feels Your Pain

I sat next to his little incubator bed and kept looking at his little body fitted with tubes. I looked at his little finger and his swollen face. I had been through a lot of pain in my life where I thought death was acceptable from the pain I had gone through, but this was a kind of pain that broke me inside like nothing in the past. This was my first born, my son, born out of my body, part of my body. I was angry, perplexed and terrified. I was too afraid to close my eyes in case he died while my eyes were closed. For some reason, I thought if I kept looking at him, he would feel me and get energy from me. I prayed that God would keep him.

I was alone, my mind was flooded with thoughts, blame, unforgiveness and anger. Oh yes, I was married. Domestic violence killed my child. I was beaten so much that it sent me into a premature labor. Beatings were the norm in my new married life instead of honeymoon and romance. I had hopes and dreams like any 18-year-old young girl. Not just a slap or two, but a fist fight, a kick fight that people usually pay money and get to see in the boxing rings. Except in my case, it was a one-sided fist and kick boxing fight. A strong man beats a young naive vulnerable 18-year-old girl brutally and mercilessly all in the name of love and leaves her to die. Then it repeats week after week. An endless dream, a bad nightmare you long to wake up from. What happens when the protector becomes the killer? Like any abusive relationships, I was isolated, no job, no money and nowhere to go. Have you ever been afraid of someone you love? You can't leave them, and you can't live with them. You go through various feelings of confusion, guilt and condemnation. I left everyone and everything for a man who promised to love and nurture and protect. I had rebelled against my parents and family to believe in the dreams that turned out to be a lie, how could I go back. He had kicked on my pregnant belly so much that I went into a premature labor in the seventh month. The doctors did their best to keep us both, and a baby boy was born. This was supposed to be a joyous occasion with celebrations but instead, my baby was fighting to live, and I could not help him. I had cried every tear, my mind was going crazy, I felt numb. I wanted to wake up from this horrible dream. The weeks that followed were filled with emotional pain indescribable. I did not feel close to God, in fact, I was angry with God.

I looked at his body struggling to live. Crying, praying, and pleading to God, I made promises and bargains, that if He spared my son's life, I would do this, or that, as we do when we are in a very traumatic place. This was my baby I held against my breast a few days ago, this was a piece of me. Days went by, I refused to leave his side or move. I longed for someone to hold me and tell me that everything was going to be alright. I was screaming on the inside, I wanted it all to just go away. I wanted someone to shake me and wake me up from this bad dream. No one wiped my tears or held me. I blamed myself for not being able to protect him. I pleaded to God as I rocked myself back and forth. He was discharged after some time but admitted again as he started turning blue. Weeks went by and his tiny body finally gave in and he died but God in His everlasting mercy, moved me away for a while so that I did not have to see him take his last breath. I was ushered to a relative's home to shower and sleep as I had not showered or slept for days. As I slept, the Lord showed me a dream where my son was waving me goodbye. He wasn't a baby. He was a little boy sitting on a swing in a lush garden full of flowers and I was pushing him from the front. He was waving at me. I was waving back. It was a very beautiful moment. I kept pushing him on the swing and he smiled and waved as I pushed him higher. I heard the phone ringing far away. Then the ringing appeared closer and louder. I felt someone shake me. I opened my eyes, and I knew that my baby boy had gone. He waved me goodbye in my dream. My heart broke. That day I changed. A part of me died with him.

I didn't cry to this day and I still do not know where my child is buried. Everything after that I still don't remember to this day, my mind blocked it. How do you get over the death of a child or a loved one? Only by God's Grace! Who can understand your pain better than God Himself, who also lost his only son, his beloved baby for us all? My testimony now brings salvation, healing, and restoration to many. Sometimes you don't get the answers you are seeking, and don't understand why, you just believe in the power greater than death. If my testimony can reach one soul and bring restoration, then my pain was not in vain.

I don't know why I had to lose my child and why God did not heal him to live with me, why I had to be broken again but one thing I know, that His love for me has not changed. He knows things I cannot understand. His ways are so much higher than my mind could fathom. I was angry with God for a long time. God alone has the power to turn your pain into a purpose as He did to me. The Bible says that Jesus was emotional at the death of Lazarus, He cried when He saw the sisters of Lazarus crying (John 11:35). He mourns with those who grieve. He was moved when he saw my heartache. He is moved when He sees your sorrow too. He is compassionate who cares about you and wants to restore what you have lost.

He holds the power to restore, to give life and He can raise even the dead things in our life that we have forgotten.

When God says to move forward, this is a very difficult task to do when your enemies are catching up and you are exhausted, your feet feel too heavy to move and there is nothing but a deep ocean in front of you. If you move forward, you will drown and if you stay you will be killed. When God has said to move forward, do we take the step into the ocean? This is a risk we must take when we move in faith. This is the blind faith the Bible talks about. When God has told you something, and you do not see a way in front of you, but you keep taking a little step forward and He opens a little door here, a subtle door there and before you know, you have come much further than you realized.

There are many heroes in the Bible who were called to do huge tasks with not much at hand. Don't you think they felt some sort of apprehension? I'm sure they felt all that we feel, fear, insecurity, not knowing how, wanting to quit, exhausted of trying and waiting, disappointed when the answer did not come when they expected it, but they did not allow the fear to stop them. They submitted their dreams and desires before God.

There is a young girl in the Bible who had her own hopes and dreams, plans for her life and one Word from God came, that messed up her plans.

Mary, the mother of Jesus had a calling in her life she did not know about. She was busy planning her wedding in a culture where weddings go on for weeks. She was happy, showing off her ring and had the glow of a young girl very much in love and about to get married. She could not stop smiling but it was short lived.

Her joy, excitement and her peace were quickly snatched from the one who prophesied to love her. God sent her His Word and in minutes the course of her life changed. The angel of the Lord came and announced to her that she was highly favored of God and was going to have a baby from the Holy Spirit who was going to envelop her.

One call, one moment with God, one encounter, one message changed her entire life.

The calling in her life was huge and so was the attack. She almost did not get married. She didn't have that joy anymore of a young bride who was longing and preparing for her grand day. She felt lonely, alone and ran to her cousin in the hope that she might understand her heart. Her calling took her out of her comfort zone, out of her home and all that which was familiar to her. Her calling announced new enemies. She was now on the run from a powerful King and she was homeless.

The calling of God will change your entire life. It will introduce you to new enemies, people will hate you and they won't even know why. Even though you may not have much to show for, they will still be jealous of you because of your calling. Mary's pregnancy catches the eye of the King who is threatened by the new unborn King. A powerful king is afraid and threatened by an unborn child.

Mary did not expect all this drama in her life. All she wanted was to get married to her man and live happily ever after. Mary was chosen to be the mother of Jesus, and she paid a price for her calling. She had no home, no picket fence, no intimacy with her man, dusty, tired and hungry, they ran for their lives. Every door they knocked rejected her. In the barn, God chose to hide the savior of the world. Some mega preachers' net worth is millions now with their vast empires, private jets and luxurious lifestyles with various mansions and expensive cars in their garages while the King of Kings was born in a place, they would not even keep their dogs.

Anytime you have an announcement of God on your life, get ready for trouble.

We love prophetic words spoken over us, but with each prophetic word is a cost attached. Nothing good comes without a fight.

The minute we accept our calling the devil will send his senior cohorts and fire his strongest bullets to distract us, put pressure on us, bring confusion, distraction till we aboard the mission.

How can a prophetic word bring so much stress and trouble? Fear not! In each encounter with God or His angel, the greeting has always been to fear not.

During adversity, God tells Moses not to be afraid, to stand firm and see the deliverance of the Lord in Exodus 14. The people were panicking and complaining to Moses in the desert when God told Moses these following simple but powerful instructions.

God had told Moses to do these 4 things at the face of his adversity:

- **Fear not** (don't be afraid, don't doubt, don't look at your adversary, look at God).

- **Be still** (stand still, don't do things on your flesh, wait on God, don't fret or complain, trust God).

- **Standby** (don't make your own plans, don't look at what's in your hand, wait on God's direction).

- **See the salvation of the Lord** (visualize it, see it happening before it happens, imagine it in your mind, observe carefully, be watchful).

Usually, when we are in trouble, we do not want to know all the details, we just want someone to get us out. But God told Moses to tell the people those 4 important tools that we all need to observe when we are facing a battle that is too big for us. We are not to be afraid or complain, or panic and do something in our flesh. Wait for direction from God and then we will see the salvation of the Lord. While we are waiting, worship Him, give Him glory and visualize the victory, see it in your mind before it happens.

When we stop whining and go to God in the first instance, instead of ringing this friend and that friend asking for their opinions about our situations, calling the church leader in fear and panic, God is the only one who can help us. We choose to share intimate details about ourselves to friends and when it has spread like fire, we have the nerve to get upset and angry because they talked. I used to also ring friends first in panic and one day as I was in the panic mode and no one was answering their phone, I was walking around meditating on the problem, thinking who should I ask, who should I call, and suddenly I heard God say, "You didn't ask me?"

From that day I have been going to God straight away. I cry to Him, complain or just sit, but He knows my heart like no other and I can trust Him.

When we are in strife and in unforgiveness, and listening to the devil's lies, the chatter stops us from hearing from God, it forms a blockage. The Bible tells us in Genesis, that God came in the coolness of the evening and called out to Adam and Eve to fellowship with them. God talks to us all the time, but we don't hear Him because of our sin and disobedience. Worry is a sin, unforgiveness, lies, and gossip are all sins, and they block us from hearing God speaking to us.

We need to be connected to God, like a plug onto the power supply, so that God can download unto us. When you get a word from God, in the form of a prophetic word or from the Bible, when it stands out to you speaking in your situation, do not allow the enemy to snatch it away from you by doubting and questioning if it was God. If you stop to ponder, the enemy will distract you with all kinds of negative thoughts and doubts and rob you of your answer.

Sometimes God will show you snippets of where He is taking you. Waiting is hard, but some things cannot be rushed. The devil will want you to do something in the flesh, rather than being still. He will tell you that maybe God forgot you or that you did not hear from God. God tells us to be still in circumstances and don't fret, "Be still and know that I am God," (Psalm 46:10).

The Bible says, "unless the Lord builds the house, they Labour in vain who builds it," Psalm 127. Waiting is hard but if you are not sure what it is that God wants you to do, it is best to wait on Him and while you are waiting, fast, pray, meditate and declare God's promise over your life. Psalm 27:14, tells us to wait on the Lord and while we are waiting, to be of good courage.

The Word of God says to put on the full armor of God (joy, praise, thanksgiving, worship, Word, speaking it), all the time, daily because our battle is daily. Problems may come but if you look closely you will see God is providing for you even in the wilderness. Others can pray for you, the pastor can pray for you, but the way you can pray about your own issues is like none other. When a woman is in a deep distress, she will be willing to sit before God till her answer came. She will not care what she looked like, if her mascara ran all over her face or if her stocking laddered, she will not care what others thought of her, all she knows is that she is desperate, and no one can help her but God. Sometimes in our lives, we must get desperate for God to move in our situations. We cannot sit on the fence and fall whichever way suits us at the time. We cannot expect God to move in our circumstances if we are not fully committed to Him. Sometimes when we are in trouble, we come running to Him but when all things are going well in our lives, we tend to forget Him. Seek Him in good times and in bad times, worship Him when all things are working great in our lives and when everything seems to fall apart, because in all things He remains God.

Unlike any other religion, our God, the God of Abraham, Isaac, and Jacob says, that we are *His* friend and He is our friend (John 15:5). We don't have to climb a hundred steps, light twenty candles and roll on the ground with metals hanging off our face like some religions do, or walk on fire, and do all sorts of religious activities to get to His presence or to get His attention. I am glad that I don't have to wash my face and hands to touch the Bible like some religions demand or having to carry my God in a bag in the form of an idol. My God carries me. He carries me in hard times, and in good times, He carries me in the storm and fire and His voice is heard under the ocean bed. All He wants from us is a relationship, not sacrifice, not religion, just a heart to love Him. When we praise Him, it activates blessings and goodness, but when we worry, it activates sickness and diseases and opens the door to the enemy to steal from us our joy and peace.

Praise Him and live. The devil does not like that God made us just a little lower than the angels (Hebrews 2:7) and crowned us with glory and honor and gave us authority over all beings including the devil. That is why he keeps us discouraged and bound up in lies. When we don't know the calling of God in our lives when we are ignorant in the Word and our purpose, we would go with anyone, and we would allow anyone to speak into us. Even though I was born again, the Word was not growing inside of me. It was not changing me, I allowed anyone to speak into me. I did not know my worth and how God saw me. It was when I found out my heritage in Christ through the Word of God, the Bible, I started to see myself through the eyes of Jesus and slowly the Word began to change my thoughts and my way of living to match the Word. I started talking to myself and to my situation just as Jesus would and slowly, I could see things in my life beginning to change. The more I spent time with God and His Word, the more my life started transforming. I was not becoming upset easily when others hurt me. My worrying decreased as my worship increased.

We can speak just like God did at the beginning of the world and call healing and restoration in our lives and the Bible says it will manifest (see Genesis), because He has given us authority over all things.

In Song of Solomon 2: 11, He is the lily of our valley, the rose of Sharon, He is the healer of our wounded bodies and the peace in the turmoil of our soul (John 14: 27), He is our daily bread in Luke 11: 3 and Matthew 6: 11, and the vine, we are the branches in John 15. He is the everlasting water (John 4: 14), and the rock (Psalm 18: 2), He is our maker (Colossians 1:16). Jesus is the living water in John 4:14 and our provider in Philippians 4:19 and He is the Alpha and Omega, the first and the last (Revelation 1:8), He is not about to forget us (Isaiah 49:15). The days when my faith is struggling, my heart feels heavy, I am not sure when and how my help will come, I look at the balance in my account and the bills looking at me, I find these scriptures and meditate on them till like fire my faith rises up and overcomes my fear. He has given us all things through His death and resurrection and promises never to leave us nor forsake us even in the latter years of our life (Job 42:12).

Chapter Thirteen
Being Like the Father

Because the devil is an imitator, he wants us to be like him. We try to imitate other people because we don't like ourselves or what we see in the mirror staring back at us. The enemy likes it when we have low self-esteem and lack confidence. With all his efforts, he remains a counterfeit, cheap imitator of God, deceiving people with his lies and half-truths, twisting the Word of God to suit his purpose. He poses to us like God and because he knows the Bible, he will even use the scriptures to test us to see how much we know. He even tested Jesus, twisting the Word of God when Jesus was coming out of fasting, so he is not about to leave us alone. He offers us a perverted copy of who God is, turning Gods Words around to suit his purpose. To be able to recognize his tactics, we need to be in the Word, in the Spirit, and in worship all the time. The Bible pronounces to us to be alert, sober in mind, because the devil, our enemy prowls around **like** a lion (not a lion but imitating like a lion), looking, searching for those who are perhaps weak in faith, whom he can devour (see 1 Peter 5:8).

That is why we need to be watchful, be vigilant, be in the Word and in prayer all the time, so that we can tell the counterfeit when he whispers into our thoughts. The devil will send his most senior demons to confuse us and keep us below our potential.

We are supposed to be Gods ambassadors declaring His Gospel of truth with everyone. When we listen to the lies of satan, and we doubt, we become ineffective in our mission of saving souls in comparison to our opponent the devil who pulls in millions of souls each second. His agents are out there working overtime. He has worked with God for a very long time, therefore he is an expert in how the

Heavenly systems work and he is very sneaky, see how well he lied to Eve in the garden of Eden in Genesis, holding a seductive conversation with her. Don't get into any conversation with the enemy, rebuke him instead. Don't get in a relationship with people you know deep down in your heart that they are not for you. When we start to chat with them, they will lead us away from God. Sometimes we look at how many people follow us on social media and work hard to get many 'likes' but God does not look at how many likes we have on the social media. He looks at our willingness, our heart, our time spent searching for Him, our hunger for Him and not by what others say about us or think about us. His love is not based on our own goodness or ability but in His strength and love.

I used to say, "Lord who will call me to preach, no one knows me, I don't carry a big-time preachers name, how will anyone find me?" Then one day I heard Him say,

"I am your Father, you have my name." It was like a penny dropped! I looked in the mirror and introduced myself saying, "I am Melvina Peka-Jehovah." I started using His surname to my name, and the more I said it, my heart started to see the new me, the big me. I started to feel big on the inside knowing that He actually was my Heavenly father. The enemy tries to bring us down by showing us how impossible our dream is, and we start seeing ourselves small as I did and when I started joining Gods name to mine, I started seeing that I had a big father who knew the entire wide world and was the CEO of the universe. He could speak to anyone anytime and launch me. He was in control. Isn't that awesome? You have a big-time father who knows which door to open for you, He knows everyone, every business, every bank, every resource, and He loves you.

Be yourself in all you do, and when you go in obedience to God, He will turn up. Our calling is different.

My experiences, my audiences are different to yours. I can't minister to you unless you too have been broken, molested, homeless, no money, been in dark lonely places because now we have something in common, pain.

Pain can draw people together. Pain can bring nations together regardless of race and color.

You see how people of all race and nationality rise to help in disasters because not one person here has been through life without some form of pain.

The pain of a loss, pain of divorce, pain of disease or terminal illness, pain of joblessness, the pain of children in alcohol and drugs can connect us with people who are also in pain.

No matter how much money we have or which side of the town we live in or what brand clothes we wear, pain will rip us apart, bring us in the darkest places but it also joins hearts because regardless of what broke us, we cry the same, we hurt the same, our tears taste the same. No one can touch our heart like another person in pain who have been through similar situations and came out on the other side.

Naomi and her two daughters-in-laws shared the commonality of pain and loss. One chose to commit to her mother in law, while one chose to go back to her idols (Book of Ruth). In life, we also get some people like that who will kiss us goodbye and walk away in our difficult times. Some friends and families will block us and turn their faces away when we need them the most. They will leave us because they don't want to be seen with us because of our shame and our loss, but God in His mercy will always give us a Ruth to walk the journey with us, who will stick with us to serve us and will commit to our calling.

We cannot go through life trying to be someone else or something that we were not called to be.

What God has given other people is not going to work for you. Don't try to be like somebody else. Don't say, "I wish I had their talent, their looks, and their personality, or their money." You will not have your testimonies and be able to fulfil your calling if you were them. You are unique and one of a kind made in God's image. God has placed inside you all you need to fulfil your task, you don't need to envy anyone else's calling.

The devil went to Jesus in the wilderness (Matthew 4), after fasting and said to Him, 'if you are the son of God, tell these stones to become bread.' Do you for one-minute think that the devil did not know who Jesus really was? And it wasn't about bread either. The enemy wanted to know if Jesus knew who He was. Do you know who you are? We can go through a life like me, condemning and judging ourselves, looking at our past, our faults and be deceived about our inheritance. Once you know who you are in Christ Jesus deep down, you will start roaring like a lion yourself.

When a woman is giving birth, she does not care about her looks, or if she has lipstick on, all she knows is that the baby is coming out and she must push. When my pushing came, I almost let it go because I started to fear. When God brings you to the front, don't apologize for it, because who God calls, He also provides for and no power in hell can stop it.

What you are going through right now is no harder than what you went through in the past. The difference is, you are in a different place, different time, different level, with a different stronger devil but you are not alone in this. Throughout the writing and editing of this book, I faced many different giants. At times it seemed like I was the only one going through such difficult times. The devil kept telling me to give up, that there was no point, but his tricks are the very same he used on Eve at the Garden of Eden. It is the same he used on Jesus asking him to turn the stones into bread. I'm here because of those lonely, teary nights when I rocked my hungry babies to sleep, lying next to them on the floor. I'm here today because people counted me out. I was discarded and humiliated, but today I praise God because there was a purpose in my pain.

Like a teabag, only when it is immersed in hot water, its flavor comes out, our hot water experience brings out the purpose of God.

Chapter Fourteen
The stones will Praise Him

A thief does not care about robbing the homeless person who sits outside a fancy department store. The thief will rob the store because the store has more valuable items than that homeless person. Likewise, the thief comes only because we have something of a great value.

We are in that trial because we have something inside of us that the devil is aware of and understands that once it is released, it will put him out of business.

It is what is inside of us that he is after, that gift, that talent, that promise, that integrity that God has given us.

What do we do when we get annoyed with the neighbour's loud pumping music every night or that dog who keeps barking each night when we go to bed and will not stop? We may endure it for some time hoping it will cease, and when it does not, there is something that rises on the inside of us ready to knock on their door. In the same way, we must put on our garment of praise and helmet of the Word and fight back, reclaim our ground that the enemy has been taking. We need to get mad enough to fight and get back our children, finances, and our health. The enemy always fights us the hardest when we are close to our victory. When we are tempted to get discouraged, and when nothing seems to be working right for us and we feel like it is never going to work out, recognize the still small voice inside of us whispering to us telling us that we in the right path to our destiny. No one is immune to the tactics of the enemy.

Every successful person had demons to fight, battles to win on the road to their success, but we don't see their flip side. The media shows us their wealth, but we did not see their tears, we haven't seen them working in takeaway shops or driving trucks on their way to fame. After many rejections, when everything around them told them to give up, they kept pushing. We all have those humble training seasons that brought us to where we are now.

When we are going through a trying time, the best thing we can do is stop talking about how big our problem is to all our friends and colleagues and start talking about how big our God is. Brag on God of His goodness and mercy telling Him how powerful and mighty He is, reminding ourselves of how he helped us in the past, that we are confident that this time He was going to bring us out also.

We have the power in our mouth to change our environment and circumstances. The Bible says in Luke 19:40 that if we keep quiet and withhold our voice, the rocks will speak. There are many negative things spoken that are out in the environment waiting to manifest in the right situation and if we do not declare and decree the Word of God over our lives, bodies and situations then those other words will manifest. In Genesis 28, we find Jacob running away from home and his angry brother. Jacob had done some wrong things that caused a division in their home. Sometimes without thinking we may say and do the wrong thing which opens the door to the enemy and then when we cannot handle the heat, we either hide from everyone or we run away as Moses and Jacob did. Our word matters, what we say and declare carry power and will manifest even years later. When we declare God's word over our environment, apply the blood of Jesus on the door posts of our homes, any demonic activities that come in our street will have to pass our home, as it did in the Bible in the Passover. In Joshua, the whole wall came down when they shouted, because our voice transfer vibrations and is alive and when spoken it can break chains and set us free from diseases and sicknesses. I went to have an operation end of 2012. I said to someone that week, that all operations had risks, and anything could go wrong, I could end up being home much longer. The operation went well but for some reason inside was not healing. I had to have many post-surgical investigations that went on for months. I was home for almost a year. I fasted and asked God why I was not getting better from a simple operation. The Lord showed me the day I had spoken those words over myself so carelessly and it had manifested what I said. Even when we say things without meaning to and it is witnessed by someone, it will manifest. Even though I repented but my words were already out. I learned that day to be careful of all my words.

I have since noticed many things in my life were a result of my negative confessions, things I had said as well as what others had said over me, and I agreed by keeping quiet instead of saying that I did not receive it in my life. Now I don't allow anyone to speak over me. If it is something I don't want to hear, I refuse it and rebuke it there and then. Someone said at work, "Oh we will probably get dementia like this when we are old." I did not agree to it. Straight away I rejected it and rebuked it in Jesus Name and decreed that I had a mind of Christ as according to the Word of God, and my memory short and long term will be intact, that God brings things to my remembrance. Be careful who you allow to speak in your life and that of your children's and your destiny. Soak your destiny in the blood of Jesus and refuse anything that is not from the Word of God, regardless of how idly or casually it has been spoken.

The houses we live in have words hanging in the air as molecules ready to be manifested. If we don't cleanse our house and speak the Word of God, rename our home as the house of God, the walls will speak what has been said over the years. Imagine the words spoken in your house before you, the fights, the tears shed, the accusations and angered words are all hanging in the air to become true. I use pure olive oil and pray over it in agreement with my husband. Then we go and put the oil in the doorpost of our house, garage door, the boundary of our home, our vehicles and the walls of our rooms and anything that has been there from before and speak the name of Jesus and declare His word of protection, rebuking all the powers of the enemy, over the spirit of death and destruction, and by the spoken Word of God we override all other words spoken in that house. I walk around a few times in the week declaring positive things in each room. Command your day; say it as you want it to be. Speak healing and restoration, speak safety over your children, speak the Blood of Jesus over yourself and everything you own, even at your workplace, in the car and while riding in the train. We are living in dangerous times, just see around us and hear the news. It is very important to declare Gods Word over everything we own and over the lives of our loved ones and prophesy our vision because if we don't the rocks, the stones and walls will speak what they have absorbed.

Chapter Fifteen
Loosed woman

As a child, I have had a relationship with God, and it was beautiful, uncomplicated and uncompromising. He was my invisible best friend, my protector and "my-everything". When you grow up in a large family, everyone compressed in a small home, you incline to discover your own space and mine was under the trees where I would build twig houses and talked to God. For me as a child God was always present, I just spoke to Him and took for granted that He was listening. God was very real to me and I told Him everything and discussed with Him everything. It was when we grow older and when life becomes complicated, we start hiding things from God. It is not that He didn't know everything about me, but I started to draw away from Him as my focus shifted from

God to boys as it does with every teenage girl. I no longer discussed things with Him openly as I did when I was younger. I guess I knew deep down what He would say, or that He perhaps would not approve of my choices. God is a father and like all fathers, He may not approve of our choices and would close the door. Most times we know the right from the wrong, but we tend to ignore His cautionary signals.

When we are young, it is easier to come to God with a childlike belief. I read the bible loud perfecting my English and performed healing services and death ceremonies on birds who fell off their perch, hurt or died or when the cat got them. When I was with God, I felt powerful, that no one could hurt me, everything appeared perfect and beautiful. All my problems subsided, insecurities departed, and I felt big in Him.

God always fixed all of my problems. I have many childhood testimonials of God's mercy in my life and how He became my best friend.

God will use our testimonies from our broken pieces to minister to the molested girl who hid in shame and lost her voice, to the girl who was raped and lived in shame losing her identity, to the mother who lost her child, and to the woman who lived in domestic violence, to the professional woman with many degrees and high profile job who hid in the secrets of her past. Life can leave you deep voids and scars that only God can fill.

Have you ever felt bent down, laden with your issues, unable to walk upright, like the lady in the Bible in Luke 13:12, who had terrible arthritis that deformed her body, she had scoliosis, she could not stand up straight? She perhaps had not seen the stars in the sky in many years, or the faces of people as she was bound up and bent over. People walked past her, but no one saw her, no one acknowledged her. Everyone was busy with their own lives. She did not miss church even though she suffered much pain, she could not walk fast, she did not see any results from her prayer, yet she continued to come in the hope that it could be any day that God would send her healing and hear her cry. No one sat with her at the back seat and all front seats were reserved for the important people. No one really stopped to offer her coffee after church. She was lonely and not only was she in physical pain but also emotional pain. She had no friends and no one who cared for her or accompanied her. Her silent tear was seen, and her prayer was heard as Jesus was at church not sitting in the front reserved seats, but at the back observing her. He saw her brokenness, her years of sacrifices and her loneliness and healed her. She walked away totally healed and restored. What a glorious day that would have been for her. How she must have praised Him for releasing her from eighteen years of pain. The same Jesus sees you today, past all that fake smile and makeup, past that insecurity and loneliness, Jesus sees through you beyond what people see. People may not have time for you and may not understand your sorrow, but God has called us all to pray for each other.

Sometimes God will lead us to a total surrender to Him through our bad choices and mistakes, sickness and diseases. The Bible says in James for us to repent to each other and pray for each other. I was sick having sudden multiple symptoms in my body for no reason.

My church friends said to me that God was punishing me for something I did wrong, that there was sin in my life, just like Jobs friends said to him (Job).

There will be times in your life when the enemy will use people to pull you down and you will feel vulnerable and question God about your circumstances and your calling.

We walk years with layers of burdens and hurts, what people have said to us, spoken about us, physical and emotional hurts, loneliness and sorrow from our past, and one encounter with Jesus, the Messiah, the healer of our broken heart, who forgives all our sins and heals our wounds, sets us free, restores all the years stolen and fills our bosom with his goodness.

As I child I enjoyed observing ants carrying things to their home. It took them quite a while to reach their destination and then they would turn around and go back to get more. The Bible in Proverbs 6 says to take a lesson from the ants that are small but wise and prepare ahead of time. The ants prepare before the winter. You see ants carrying things all the time.

When there is an announcement of a storm coming or a hurricane, we always prepare. I grew up in Fiji where we often had hurricanes. I saw my parents and neighbours prepare for the storm by securing their roofs and homes, buying candles, matches, kerosene for lamps, storing water and canned food items.

It was preparation time for what was coming ahead. It is one thing to trust in God when all is going well in our lives, but when all resources die, when all our friends leave, when we are in a bad place, it is not so easy to trust but that is the most important time to hang onto God. It is the time we are tested, everything you have ever learned is put in the test.

Most of us look at our sickness and diseases, our downtime as if it is permanent. Downtime is the time when nothing seems to be working in our life. The lady who was sick for eighteen long years continued to seek God regardless of what her body told her.

When we seek God's wisdom and put Him first in our lives and in everything we do, He takes care of everything else.

Psalm 138 speaks of David's heart, "Though I am surrounded by troubles, you will bring me safely through. Your fist is clenched against my enemies. Your power will save me."

Maybe you feel like David today. You're surrounded by all kinds of troubles, sickness, joblessness, divorce, marriage issues, addictions issues, difficulties of different kinds. Maybe you are tempted to just settle right there, in your trouble zone, make a tent and say I can't do this, I can't go any further, it's too hard.

Maybe you feel like you have been wandering homeless in the desert hungry, thirsty and feeling faint or perhaps the waves high and pounding hard around you and you fear to sink? Is your appetite gone and your days are filled with anxiety and tears?

Most of us have been down that gravelled road barefooted more than once in our lives. If you are feeling challenged at work or in your personal life and the world seems to be against you, reaching out to God could be your only answer. Jesus died and rose, loosing us from all our troubles and from all those things we have been holding onto for years, all we must do is to receive Him. He is saying to you, Woman thou art loosed (Luke 13:12).

Chapter Sixteen
The Fragrance of the Broken

From my heart to you, you might be the girl God inspired me to write this book for, this message is ministering to a broken girl like me, who yearned for love and looked for it everywhere and because I did not know my worth, I went with someone the enemy sent to break me and steal my promise or you could be the young mother or father who is grieving a baby or the person in domestic violence.

When we put everything into a relationship and we lose it, we learn to fight, to endure, and to love unconditionally. We may have become wounded and weak but love costs, it takes our all to love someone the way God loves us. Sometimes we feel vulnerable, we may hate them for hurting us, but we are not able to leave because in some strange way we love them and need them. I survived the harsh realities of life to share with you my story. Maybe your story is tougher than mine had been but when we show our scar to another, we pull our sleeves up and show the needle marks of our dark days, we show them our bravery. We allow our scar to speak to their dark place and lead them to the Blood of Jesus.

"The sun of Righteousness will rise in your story as my God rides with healing in His wings (Malachi 4:2).

My scar is before me every day. It follows me everywhere and is part of my life. I cannot scrape it away, tattoo over it or hide it. I tried to keep it hidden from others as I thought it was ugly. I was ashamed of it and ashamed of what it represented. Then one day Jesus showed me something that changed my perception, changed my self-worth, changed my life. Jesus showed me His scar. And in His scar, was me. I saw my brokenness, my tears, my sorrows, my hopelessness, and my broken heart. In his scar,

I saw the shame of my abuse, the death of my child, my torn, bloodied, beaten and broken body that was left to die. In his scar, I saw my dead dreams, my rejections, and my failures. I saw the blood of Jesus pouring over all my shame, my rejections, and my hopelessness. I watched it flow to my gaping wounds that were refusing to heal, cleansing it and closing it like a wound being sutured by the master hands of a physician. I saw His light taking over the darkness in my life. As I watched I felt hope returning, I saw my tears dropping into his hands like pearl crystals that still bore the mark of the nails. I felt His scarred hand resting on me, and His strength in my weakness. I saw my own scar through His eyes for the first time and this time I saw a strong woman who was resilient. I saw a woman who fought battles and won, a woman who led her children through the hot desert and wilderness, a brave woman who killed Goliath and stomped on scorpions. I saw a very precious woman who walked with her head held high like an exquisite silk flowing freely in the breeze. I saw all this in Jesus' scar. Then I finally realized this is how God saw me. That day my life changed. I truly felt born again. This was my new life. It isn't just a scar. It is a trophy, a sign of victory, a seal of healing, a signpost, a landmark. I see the broken pieces of my life carefully put together to form a beautiful exquisite mosaic. I now understand that my pain was never in vain. It was the flip side of my purpose. You could not separate one from another. Now I Praise Him as my scar is a reminder of the battles my God helped me fight and win. My scar reminds me of the Blood of Jesus that was shed for me, "But he was pierced for our transgressions, he was crushed for our iniquities; the punishment that brought us peace was on him, and by his wounds, we are healed," (Isaiah 53:5 NIV). Those of us who feel alone, shamed and discarded like a dirty cloth, my scar empowers them and helps them see themselves through the eyes of Jesus. My scar is my shadow. I cannot scrape it away. I cannot tear it from me. It is part of me, it is my strength, it reminds me of the scar on Jesus' hand and on Jesus side. I am no longer ashamed of my scar, I now wear it as my bravery medal to remind me of who I am in Christ Jesus.

Whatever you have come out off, remember Jesus' opinion is the only opinion that matters, and He said to the woman caught in adultery, "I also don't condemn you, go and sin no more," (John 8:1-11).

He loves you and cares for you

Wear the scar of your past as a testimony to encourage others. It is to remind you of who you were once and where God found you. It will remind you that you can shine the brightest wherever you are, and you don't need anyone's validation or endorsement. My scar reminds me of the many lessons I learnt through the pain of my life, each time the abuser's boot kicked my pregnant stomach, each time my face was broken, and each time I was flung across the floor. In the dark cold floor, I was not alone; there was someone mightier who was collecting my blood drops and my tears. It brought me back to my childhood friend, my God, it made me stronger and wiser, and it taught me forgiveness. "For you, O Lord, are my hope, my trust, O LORD, from my youth," (Psalm 71:5).

In the death of my child, when my heart hurt, I saw God's heart, "For God so loved the world that he gave his one and only Son, that whoever believes in him shall not perish but have eternal life," John 3:16 NIV.

My pain had a purpose far beyond what I could have understood at that time. In my pain, God had the names of many souls hidden who my scar would minister to. It takes a lot to speak about your pain, it is like re-living every detail that you want to bury, but unless you face the giant, it will keep whispering to you from the past.

About the Author

Melvina is called to be an Evangelist from a very young age. Her loving, transparent and positive attitude has brought many souls to the Lord.

Melvina is the youngest daughter of twelve children, known to her family as Alli, grew up in Fiji, in a strong Christian family. At that time her family was the only Christian family in the village. As a child, Melvina had no friends and often felt rejected and lonely and tried hard to fit in. She made Jesus her 'best friend' and that is what she called Him and spent many hours talking and 'hanging out' with him. Her ministry started when she travelled to the village with missionaries. She was only 11 years old when she commanded demons to come out of a young mentally ill girl in the village.

Melvina made some poor decisions that took her away from God and caused her much heartache.

Melvina is now showing others her life scars and helping many like her through her testimonies. She helps other women who have been abused, rejected and labelled, to fight their fears and insecurities and rise to Gods plan for their lives.

Melvina is determined to be the voice that comforts you and brings you hope and love.

"Comfort, says our God. Comfort them! "Isaiah 40:1 **GNT**

Praise

"Lord, you are my God;

I will exalt you and praise your name,

For in perfect faithfulness

You have done wonderful things.

Things planned long ago." Isaiah 25:1 NIV.

"My mouth is filled with your praise declaring your splendor all day long." Psalm 71:8 NIV.

"Sing to God; sing in praise of His Name,

Extol Him who rides on the clouds;

Rejoice before Him – His name is the Lord."

Psalm 64:4 NIV.

Accepting Jesus

If you have tried everything and still feel empty inside, alone and searching for answers, I would like to introduce Jesus to you, who came looking for me when I was hiding in shame, hopelessness and in fear.

Jesus who is the son of God and all power and authority over everything in Heaven and on Earth has been given to Him and in Whose Name every knee must bow. To come to God, we must come via Jesus. To become born again is to accept Jesus in your heart as the Bible says in Romans 10: 9-10 ESV, "If you confess with your mouth that Jesus is Lord and believe in your heart that God raised him from the dead, you will be saved. For with the heart one believes and is justified, and with the mouth, one confesses and is saved".

Repeat this prayer with your mouth, so that your ears can hear it.

"Lord Jesus, I believe in my heart and declare with my mouth you are Lord Jesus, the son of God and you died for me. I believe you arose, and you are sitting at the right hand of God pleading for me. I accept you as my Lord and my Saviour. Make something of me. Fill me with our Holy Spirit. In Jesus Name, Amen."

Now you are born again. Jesus has come inside of you in spirit and will help and restore your life as He did mine.

Find a charismatic church who believe in Father, Son and Holy Ghost and become part of the movement sharing the gospel of Christ and becoming all that God has called you to be.

Download your own personal FREE scripture meditation booklet here or send us an email;

Broken To Restored

melvinaministry@gmail.com

https://documentcloud.adobe.com/link/track?uri=urn%3Aaaid%3Ascds%3AUS%3A7bcdbb72-f1c8-4b89-9032-7e7c5cb6d860

Membership Form

Please complete this application to join Mel's community so you can be reminded of FREE products and promotions.

First Name _____

Last Name _____

Cell Phone _____ Work Phone _____

Email _____

Country & City _____

Please scan and email to melvinaministry@gmail.com

https://www.instagram.com/melvinapeka/
https://twitter.com/melvinapeka?s=09
https://www.melvinapekaministries.com/mels-blogs
https://m.facebook.com/melvinapekaministries/
https://www.youtube.com/channel/UCKN3_bea0oEd3sH0d4qJXGg

www.ingramcontent.com/pod-product-compliance
Lightning Source LLC
Chambersburg PA
CBHW032025290426
44110CB00012B/679